THE GIFT OF
HOME

BRE DOUCETTE

TEN PEAKS PRESS™
EUGENE, OR

To Jesse,

For always being the safe place where I belong.

Thank you for putting up with every project and crazy idea I've had. For allowing my creative passion to run free inside our four walls. For not always getting the credit you deserve, even though you are the true muscle behind my madness. These projects couldn't come to life without your knowledge and skills.

To you, Carter and Dannika,

You are my inspiration and driving force to create welcoming spaces wherever we call home.

CONTENTS

The ache for home is in all of us. The safe place where we can go as we are + not be questioned.

Maya Angelou

LOVE THE SPACE
YOU LIVE IN

The ache for home lives in all of us.
— **Maya Angelou**

God put the desire for home into each one of us. It is no surprise that we seek the feeling of belonging and love in the places we live and are eager to share that sense of home with our family and friends.

But what happens when you lose that sparkle in your eyes for the spaces you call home because life got busy, you got a new job, you had a new baby, or your babies grew up and moved out? (Or back in!) Whatever season of life you are experiencing, I'm here to encourage you.

I believe that anyone can *love the space they live in*. This idea came to life nearly a decade ago when I brainstormed the message I wanted my blog to be about. It's a motto I have used for my life and when helping friends and clients design spaces in their homes.

Starting can be the hardest part. With all the options and home remodeling shows, it is easy to become impatient or experience decorating-decision paralysis—as if the decorating police are going to come tell us we've done it all wrong.

I'm here to help you exhale all the decorating anxieties that might be holding you back and to encourage you to inhale all the possibilities of truly loving the space you are in. I use my home as the example, but this book is ultimately about finding a way to your sanctuary and your vision while loving what surrounds you today.

I know. It's much easier to point out the things we don't love. The outdated tile, the toilet that needs to be replaced, the worn-out recliner in the living room, or the dingy carpet you are desperate to swap for beautiful hardwood floors. (You know . . . the carpet bearing the forever stain from your daughter's spilled nail polish. Just me? I digress.) I'll admit I've been guilty of walking around our home—this home that I prayed for, mind you—grumbling about all it lacked. That wish list of to-dos left me full of discontentment. But the moment I turn my complaining into appreciation, my heart is once again filled with thanksgiving for our home, slanted walls and all.

The secret is to love our homes right now—imperfections and all—while creating beauty on any budget, under any circumstances, so we can refresh ourselves and others starting today.

I promise you, the blessings that emerge in a home prepared with love and attention are never limited by square footage or a lack of trendy furniture. God doesn't require us to be perfect—he encourages us and guides us to offer our gifts to others. In the same way, we certainly don't have to wait until our homes are perfect before they become a place to welcome, gather, nourish, refresh, grow, serve, create, and experience beauty.

The following sections introduce you to the topics we'll explore in this tour of rooms. Along the way, my deepest hope is that you will encounter ideas, encouragement, and simple solutions to reignite your love for and appreciation of home no matter the season of life.

I'm so glad you are here.

BRE'S DECOR
and more GUIDE

{ Getting Started }

When I was a young girl, you could often find me redecorating my bedroom after school. I spent hours rearranging my furniture and my few accessories and knickknacks. I moved everything around like it was a master chess game, and I didn't stop until I loved the look.

The best part? My creativity ran free and unchecked!

I was free to follow my instincts without worrying about rules or shoulds or "what not to do" articles. I could try different vignettes, and if I didn't like one, I didn't consider it a mistake, because I was that much closer to what felt right, what felt like home. I have carried that same principle into decorating our home today . . . which means the following advice and tips are not bottom-line rules. No way, not here. They are offerings I pray will set you free to enjoy your journey!

Embrace Your Look

I started using the term "farmhouse" to describe my decorating style far before it was an actual design style. The truth is that to me, "farmhouse" didn't represent a style as much as it represented all the ways I wanted my home to feel. Comfortable. Like going to Grandma's house when I was a kid. Relaxing. Time-worn pieces that encourage you to let down your guard without fearing a spill. Inviting. Cozy enough to make you want to curl up with a good book or breathe out all your cares from the day. Engaging. Surrounded with warm memories tied to family heirlooms and photos.

When put on the spot to define my style, I started saying, "If *Country Living* magazine and Pottery Barn had a baby, it would probably look like my home." Rather than forcing myself into a single design style category, I freed myself to explore decor options and choose what I loved, without worrying about messing up or having an exact label. Here are three ideas that might help you define your own style.

Follow the feelings. Once I identified the feelings I wanted my home to evoke—comfortable, relaxing, inviting, engaging—I made choices with greater ease. Jot down the feelings you want your home to inspire. Playful, energetic, warm, inviting, serene, casual, elegant, relaxed? Once you've identified your top three to five words, keep them handy for reference at every step.

Look at what you love. Use Pinterest or Houzz boards or go retro and create a design dream board with cut-out photos, fabric samples, paint color strips, and other inspirations. Compile pictures of rooms that say "home" to you. Identify similarities between the spaces. I did this and noticed three common threads: All the images had white walls, jute rugs, and reclaimed wood. I knew I needed to incorporate those into my family's spaces.

Pay attention to your wardrobe. Yep, you read that right. A design tip I offer my clients and my blog community at *Rooms for Rent* is to describe their favorite outfit as a way to understand their design style. Use me for example!

My favorite outfit is a pair of worn-in jeans with a plain white top, and usually I'm barefoot. Nothing is as relaxing as a favorite pair of distressed jeans (that feel more like sweatpants) and the simplicity of a white top. I'm not much of a jewelry person, but my favorite pieces are costume jewelry made from unfinished wooden beads.

I'll never forget the first time I met one of my fellow bloggers at a conference. She commented on how my outfit perfectly reflected my home decor. I was "wearing my house" (her words, not mine), and it showed me just how important it is to immerse ourselves in things we love whether we're dressing or decorating.

Following the clues in my closet, all my white blouses and T-shirts give away my love for decorating with white! And those distressed jeans reveal my preference for relaxed, casual furnishings. My wooden necklace reflects my love of textured and natural accessories and pieces, like wooden picture frames and furniture.

Try it! What colors, shades, or patterns appear in your favorite outfits? Is your daily attire a bit relaxed or a bit more elegant? Do you love to go bold or be subtle? Which characteristics of your fashion look are already in your home decor? Which could be added to a room to help you love the space you live in?

Seven Design Elements

Here are seven foundational design elements. These provide a checklist of sorts to guide and inspire your choices. As we go through each of the rooms, I will explore which three elements I focused on. I hope this helps you know you can start simple and end with great results.

COLOR PALETTE

Choosing the right color palette for my space is almost always about the emotions inspired by the color. Color sets the mood for the room, and the emotions we feel when we are in that space. The color palette in your room is depicted by not only the color on the walls but also the hues of the fabrics and accessories you use to decorate. Whether you prefer spaces with deep, bold colors or light, neutral ones, I'll share with you my tips for creating a cohesive look throughout your whole house as we go through each room.

TEXTURE + LAYERING

If you have been a frequent visitor to my blog, then it's no secret that I love incorporating texture and layers into any space. I believe texture is as important as color in creating a space you love. Texture can show up in lots of places, such as distressed furniture, warm wood tones, and woven fixtures like baskets or bamboo shades. It is a key element for adding warmth to a space, and there's nothing I love more than layering it in with variety. Layers add depth and give your room dimension.

ACCESSORIES + STYLING

Accessories allow our homes to tell our story. They are the personal accents, travel mementos, or the little quirky items that captured our attention in our most recent stroll through HomeGoods. Accessories add character to our spaces and offer us the chance to add some detail and interest in little and big ways throughout our home. I'll offer tips for incorporating the right amount of accessories and show you how to style them to add your own personal touch while highlighting your personality and story.

FURNITURE

I have discovered that I much prefer the look and feel of a room with furniture pieces that have been acquired over time. The process takes a little longer than when buying a complete set at a

furniture store, but there's something so exciting about hunting for just the right pieces that allow your spaces to feel complete and completely like you.

Furniture serves us by offering function and comfort in each room, yet our selections also showcase our personal style. Think of your furniture as your wardrobe staples. My bigger pieces of furniture are classic and lean toward neutral, which allows me to change my decor (you know, the jewelry and accessories in an outfit) seasonally or as the mood strikes. I buy key pieces first—a bed or the sofa—and then add in accent pieces or treasures I find over time. By mixing and matching furniture, we allow spaces to come alive, each piece with its own story to tell.

ARCHITECTURAL DETAILS

Adding dimension and character to a room with architectural details will add some oomph to an otherwise plain space. Does your home feel like a cookie-cutter version of others in your neighborhood? Do your walls feel flat in the space? The improvements we've made in our own 1846 farmhouse have brought back some of the original charm to plain walls that didn't feel warm and cozy. Shiplap, wainscoting, moldings, and trim work around doors provide personality, warmth, and texture. And don't forget about the ceiling! Often referred to as the fifth wall in the room, ceilings are a great surface for beadboard, planked wood, or wood beams.

LIGHTING

Lighting is the key to creating a welcoming and functional space. Just about every room is equipped with one overhead light, but I will tell you right now, those aren't my personal favorites. While having the right amount of light can support the room's purpose, choosing the right lighting will add ambience, beauty, and style as well. Chandeliers and pendant lights are a great way to add a personal touch to a space, while table lamps and floor lamps help a room feel intimate and cozy.

TEXTILES + FABRICS

Choosing textiles and fabrics to add visual interest is a creative, satisfying venture. We can showcase our unique style through those choices—from rugs and curtains, to the fabrics we pick for our upholstery and accessories. They add interest to a space and offer a warm embrace to all who enter. They also offer practicality in decorating for whatever season of life we are in. Patterns and materials play a part in the overall design scheme of your home and can highlight one design style over the next depending on the finishes that speak to you.

The Family-Friendly Home

I could have a pristine home that looks like it belongs in a high-end magazine, but if my family doesn't feel welcome and comfortable, then I have missed the mark. In each chapter I'll share ways you can keep your spaces family friendly.

Your home's decor is your chance to tell your family's story. Choose decor that resonates with you, reflects memories of loved ones, or reminds you of shared family experiences. We love our summer trips to the beach and the souvenirs we gather there. During the winter, those displayed treasures remind us of summer days and digging our toes in the sand.

When you create your spaces, don't lock everything away in fear of things getting broken or stained. Use what you love. I don't want my home to be without my white slip-covered sofa. (More about that epiphany in the living room chapter!) Creative solutions allow you and me to design beautiful homes that suit *us*.

Your sanctuary is for your entire family. If your living room floor is covered with toys, it's only temporary. This season will pass, and soon those tiny people won't be little anymore. Savor this time and find what works. In many rooms, I'll point out

organization ideas that prevent our family's stuff from taking over the function and beauty of a space.

When I look around our home, I smile knowing that the way each nook and each room is decorated truly reflects the people who live inside it and us as a family. A family-friendly approach ensures that your designed spaces will reflect the people and what is important to them. We'll explore just how to do that so when members of your family enter a room, they feel comfort and grace and love.

The Gift of a Budget

I love hunting through the clearance aisles for home decor items. One of my favorite finds, and how I came up with the name for my blog, came from a discounted item. Pottery Barn was typically beyond my budget, but one day I stumbled across their clearance section online. Among its affordable temptations was a large wooden sign that looked like it came from an old mercantile store. It read, "Rooms for Rent." It had the vintage look and tones I loved ... and was 90 percent off! I quickly put it in my purchase cart.

I named my blog after that sign because I wanted to give others decorating ideas they could "rent" for their own rooms. Ideas are the best reusable resource! Make them your own. Give them the places in your life and home that serve you and your home without spending a lot of money doing it.

Budgets get a bad rap, but they are gifts. When we have a realistic idea of how much we can spend, we make better decisions and keep our wallets and hearts in check. Allow your available resources to dictate which areas you tackle first, and then save for the bigger future projects.

Even though I have been lucky enough to maintain a home decor blog, I still plan and budget for any room refresh or makeover we hope to do. I installed peel-and-stick tiles from the dollar store when we rented. I've decorated with curbside or thrift-store finds and spruced up hand-me-down treasures. Still do. And this book shows evidence of my other way of saving . . .

. . . my DIY adventures. I wouldn't trade the journey of successes or missteps for anything. To inspire your adventure, I share a DIY in each chapter. Try them. Change them up. Or use them for inspiration to tackle your projects.

If you are new to DIYs, build your confidence. Begin small (save refinishing that family heirloom for later), have all the tools and supplies ready, count any mishaps as perfect training, and pace yourself. I'm notorious for starting too many projects at once, while my husband prefers that we stick to one at a time. He's helped me learn the value of balance. You and I don't always need a project going on in order to be loving our home. (But there's no harm in daydreaming about the next one, right?)

Along this journey, I'll mention ways to save money and enjoy the gift of your budget. Don't make it about limiting funds, but about stretching the fun of being resourceful and creative.

———————

As you and I tour our homes room by room, we'll explore where and how to get started in each space so you can stay motivated and true to your end goal. Together we can love the spaces we live in and enjoy the many gifts of home.

THE
LIVING ROOM

{ A Place to Feel Welcome }

There's lots of talk about kitchens being the center of a house, but the living room is the heart of our family's home. I hear it in my son's voice when he's sitting in his favorite chair and sharing how much he loves to be in his favorite spot. It's a gift to feel truly welcomed and at home in a space, one we get to enjoy and one that offers the gift of refreshment to everyone else who enters the space as well.

It's the place where we come together and share so many great moments. This is where we have family movie night with popcorn and peanut M&M's, enjoy lazy Sunday afternoons watching football, plop down for afternoon naps, and spend the occasional "date night in" with takeout on the coffee table.

Life happens in our living room. We've shared laughs with friends, had intimate conversations over giant cups of coffee, held Bible studies, and so much more. Our house doesn't have a family room, so this room even served as the playroom when our kids were toddlers. Toys were sometimes strewn all over the floor, and now that the kids are older, it's where we have ultimate LEGO challenges and intense games of Uno.

This is where my family feels at home.

Everybody has their favorite spot. Mine is a cozy corner of our couch, where my coffee can rest within reach on a side table. My husband and our son have dubbed the two side chairs in our living room as their personal thrones. Our daughter prefers throwing herself on a mile-high pile of throw pillows on the floor to unwind at the end of the day.

Because of its importance to all of us, I've spent much time designing our living room and tweaking it to make the space feel just right. I don't want our living room merely to look nice; I want it to tell our story and be an authentic representation of the life we have created. To do this, I focused on flooring and textiles that suited my style, colors and tones to follow my heart, and textures and layers to bring warmth to my neutral palette. My hope is that by sharing my process, I can help you create the feeling you are after and express the story of your family and home.

As a good reminder for you and me, the living rooms in which I've felt most welcomed weren't decorated to perfection, grandiose in size or feel, or all one certain style. The common thread is that they were comfortable. Approachable.

When our living rooms reflect us and our hope for others, they provide an invitation for everyone to be themselves and to stay longer than they intended.

Where to Start

Whether your living room is made up of hand-me-down furniture, pieces collected over time, or a complete set from the local furniture store, I'm going to show you how you can create a living room you long to be in.

Determine what you want to be your focal point. Not sure? Think about the purpose for your living room. Is it for gathering with friends over drinks around the fireplace? Or movie night

BY WISDOM A HOUSE
IS BUILT AND THROUGH
UNDERSTANDING IT
IS ESTABLISHED;
THROUGH KNOWLEDGE
ITS ROOMS ARE FILLED
WITH RARE AND
BEAUTIFUL TREASURES
PROVERBS 24:3

with the family? Or perhaps you have a beautiful view and a wall full of windows where you can sit and gaze for hours.

In our living room, the longest wall is also the first one you see when you walk in. I created a focal point by centering the sofa between the two curtained windows. However, something was still missing. While browsing through HomeGoods one day, I found a large, round, wooden mirror. I loved the scalloped edges and weathered wood finish. Placed above the sofa, it created the much-needed focal point you see in our living room today.

Whether it's a fireplace, the TV, a window, artwork, a favorite architectural piece, or a round wooden mirror, arranging your furniture with a focal point will help the space feel grounded and defined.

The Beauty of a Mistake
{Textiles + Fabrics}

Our living room hasn't always been the soft, neutral space it is today. If you followed my blog in those early days, you know this to be true. Our living room used to have brightly colored walls and bold patterns throughout. At the time, I let others convince me that I couldn't decorate with white because I had toddlers. Fearfully I heeded their advice. That was mistake number one. We had navy-blue slipcovers on our furniture, deep red and sage-green throw pillows, and black accessories. And our living room walls were painted Wasabi Powder . . . yes, like the insanely hot, green paste you get when you order sushi.

We needed a new area rug for our living room, and I took the opportunity to dive headfirst into the design trends other bloggers were choosing and purchased a dark navy-blue and white Moroccan trellis rug for $300. I was excited to own something on trend, but from the moment I unrolled that rug, I knew in my gut it was a mistake.

I convinced myself that something so pretty couldn't be bad. That was mistake number two. Trying to make the rug work,

TIP

Not every living room has a focal point, so don't worry if yours isn't noticeable. Take some time to think it through and identify the place that feels most natural to you.

I brought in accessories that matched it. Bold navy-blue and white chevron-stripe pillow covers (also on trend) didn't solve anything. The rug still seemed to swallow our living room whole.

A year later, I was still unable to admit defeat. So I turned next to our wall color. Maybe that would save this space. I picked out Halo by Benjamin Moore, a barely there shade of off-white, because I was still too afraid to override the advice and opinions of others and go for a true white. That was mistake number three. The lighter walls made the dark colors and bold patterns of the rug and accessories speak even louder. Another few months passed before I confessed to my husband that I didn't like the rug. His solution was simple: Sell it. He said that he didn't really care what we had for a rug as long as we had one where our active, crawling children played.

His response gave me the freedom I needed. In decor and life, you can't move on from a problem until you admit there is one. However, even though the rug was a problem, I realized that it wasn't a regrettable mistake because I learned so much about my style while trying to make it work. I learned it's okay to like something and yet not buy every pretty trend that scrolls by. And I learned that I should never let somebody who doesn't live in my home determine how I decorate it. My friend, you have to love it, because at the end of the day, you are the one who has to live with it.

Look at your own flooring. Does it express the style you want? After my adventure, I still believe area rugs can be the key to anchoring the furniture and transforming a space. Even if you have carpet, area rugs add style and layers, which I share more about later in this chapter.

If you aren't sure what size of rug to buy, measure your space! Common rug sizes are 5 x 7, 6 x 9, and 8 x 10. If the rug is too small, it will feel awkward or so underwhelming it does nothing. If a rug is too large, it consumes all the attention. A general rule is to get a rug large enough that the two front feet of your sofa or armchairs are placed on the rug.

As for style and pattern, that is a personal choice. Learn from my mistake—think it through and be true to you. If you like neutral patterns and soft tones, then perhaps a jute rug is best. If you love patterns and bold colors, decide if you want your rug to express those and potentially become the focal point or whether you want to bring in color through accessories.

Don't be afraid to take chances. After all, even a mistake is an invitation to learn more about our style and grow as we continue to decorate homes we love.

Getting Neutrals Right
{Color Palette}

I have always been drawn to white slipcovered sofas. It's no secret. And considering my favorite outfit to wear and my love for wearing white, it is no surprise that I have a white couch. I love how bright and crisp it makes our living room. And how I can easily change up the throw pillows if I want to modify the look or mood.

Once the boldly patterned area rug was gone, I went back to the drawing board, this time determined not to make another costly mistake. I surveyed my inspiration photos of the living rooms I loved, and I wrote down all the colors that recurred in those spaces. I noticed that among all the white, every single room had a jute rug. I love that jute rugs are durable for high-traffic areas and add much-needed texture to balance out the white.

To make sure that neutral spaces don't become boring, add warmth and visual depth with texture. One happy way to do this is with baskets, which are also handy for keeping throw blankets nearby or tucking toys out of sight. Plants add creation's neutral tones. Distressed wood tones—perhaps in wooden candlesticks or chippy pieces of furniture—also make rooms feel cozy. I used a cedar chest as our coffee table. The warm, rich wood tones contrast with the white. This piece, built by my husband's grandfather, adds gentle warmth to my

---

TIP

Remember to stay true to you. Advice from friends can be helpful, but at the end of the day, you are the one living there, so create a space you truly love.

neutral interior and also honors our family's story. Incorporating antique pieces, whether they come from your family or not, is a great way to add character and texture through their distressed finish. You can't help but wonder about the story they carry with them.

I like to choose three main colors to repeat throughout our living room for a cohesive look. White, wood tones, and shades of blue are repeated throughout our entire first floor to keep one's gaze moving throughout with ease.

For even more variation in my neutral palette, I turn to another one of my favorites—stripes. I add them with throw pillow covers, curtains, rugs, and accessories. Once you identify the colors and the patterns you are drawn to most, you can go about decorating your living room more freely, knowing you are making choices based off of your particular design style. Whether your couch is white, like mine, or forest green, choosing your anchor furniture in colors and tones that speak to you will allow your personal style to come through.

Yes, I made the mistake of incorporating bold patterns even though I desired the calm of neutrals. But the truth is that I've also made the mistake of going too white as well, leaving our space feeling stark and cold. So whenever I'm getting away from the true north of my taste and my hopes, I go back to my inspiration images to see if a choice I made is leading my style astray or if something is missing that my heart longs for.

Do right by your heart and trust your gut. You will know when you are on the right track because it will feel just right, giving you the ultimate sense of home.

Achieving Dimension and Warmth
{Textures + Layers}

You can paint the perfect color on your walls and have all your favorite accessories, but without layers, the room can end up

feeling flat. Layers can show up in many different forms. Area rugs, window treatments, and throw pillows are great places to start. When I first started looking around our living room for areas to improve and then compared my space to my inspiration photos, I noticed that all the windows in the images I liked had woven blinds paired with single-panel curtains that hung to the floor. I couldn't afford custom blinds, but I could afford wooden bamboo blinds from the home improvement store. Hanging them in our living room added not only layers but warmth too.

One of my favorite ways to add layers is with throw pillows. My go-to throw pillow sizes are 22, 20, or 18 inches. I like lumbar throw pillows too. A combination of sizes and shapes will naturally present layers and give more interest to the space. I also love the look of layered area rugs or an area rug on top of a carpet. (Yes, I firmly believe you can use an area rug even if you have wall-to-wall carpet!) If buying two area rugs at the same time might feel costly, a more budget-friendly way to layer area rugs is to purchase your larger area rug first and then save up for the smaller area rug for the top layer. Currently in our living room, we have an 8 x 10 jute rug with a 5 x 8 striped rug layered on top. This arrangement presents texture and introduces pattern into our living room in a simple way.

Layers can be added visually. For example, I pay attention to the placement of my table lamps on each side table. I place them just slightly in front of the artwork hanging on the wall behind them to create a layered look. I like my artwork to look as though it's peeking out from behind the lamp. This draws attention to the art, making one want to take a step farther into the room to see more. When you see everything right away in a room, you miss the opportunity for the beauty of a space to unfold. Let your guests discover different special moments in a room, and they will feel more delighted by the space and welcomed into it.

Of course, layers can be added tangibly as well. By including different textures in your decor choices, you invite others to

reach out and touch something in the space. I love it when someone comes over and, without even thinking, they reach for a wool blanket draped on the couch, or they run their fingers over a glass bowl.

For the most dimension and appeal, include three different textures into your living room. To accomplish this, you can include both smooth and distressed, shiny and soft. You can also incorporate different materials, such as wood, glass, metal, and wicker. Even your fabric can provide various textures, such as a rough woven linen or a soft wool. From the fabric choices you make to the accessories you bring in, you have opportunities to welcome different textures into your living room and create dimension that welcomes family and friends to find beauty, comfort, and refreshment in your home.

The Family-Friendly Living Room

After we had our first child, people told me a white couch would be impractical. Wanting a family-friendly home, I took the white slipcovers off of our IKEA couch and replaced them with a navy-blue ticking-stripe slipcover.

By the time baby number two came, my living room was littered with toys. I was longing for it to feel like me again . . . back before all the Fisher-Price toys and tiny humans invaded. I considered adding throw pillows, but those would just become landing pads for our kids' cannonballs. Could I style our coffee table with a vase and flowers? Nope—the baby would pull those down. I was stuck . . . until the next time I had to wash the blue covers. I removed them and faced reality—I missed the white. I hurried downstairs and pulled the white slipcovers out from the storage. "Hello, my old friends."

The moment I put them on, I was refreshed. And I decided I didn't care how many times kids spilled chocolate milk on them— never again would I exile them to the basement. Spills happen,

STYLE A COFFEE TABLE WITH LAYERS

Add personality, texture, and layers to your coffee table in no time! Surface-area vignettes are enjoyable to create, gaze at, and rearrange when you're ready for a small change with surprising impact.

1 Place a tray—rectangular or circular—in the center of your table. The defined parameters make styling simpler, keep objects organized, and visually ground the vignette. Trays also make it easy to clear off your table quickly when little ones play or dinner is served in front of the TV.

2 Layer larger items first, such as coffee table books or a large vase. I stack at least two large coffee table books toward one side of my tray, leaving room on the other for a large vase or plant.

3 Add in a natural element. Fresh flowers or a plant will introduce height, natural texture, color, and life into the space.

4 Top it off with a knickknack. I often place one on top of the stacked books. This is an embellishment to your vignette. A shiny object or glass candle votive offers a little sparkle. I've also used smaller picture frames or tiny objects I gathered when traveling. Consider what showcases your style while adding a unique shape. To avoid clutter, I usually limit it to one or two knickknacks.

5 Repeat. Style your table anew every season or when your room needs a refresh.

and slipcovers are meant to be washed. The imagined disaster turned into the right decision for me and my family. You can have a family without sacrificing your happy place. Simply choose options that serve your season and style.

- ◆ Do you love linen but don't trust your family with it? Incorporate it in throw pillows and curtains and out-of-reach surfaces.

- ◆ Be realistic about your family's wear and tear on furniture. Choose pieces knowing whether they are for a particular life season or for the long haul.

- ◆ Select storage pieces that complement your style and allow all toys to be stashed away. I invested in large, pretty baskets.

Your family longs for a place to be welcomed, so don't be surprised if you find them spending more time in your living room once you've taken the steps to make it into a space that you love.

BRE'S TOP 10
ESSENTIALS

Throw pillows

Area rug

Layered window treatments

Personal artwork

Storage baskets

Table lamps

Greenery

Candles

Coffee table tray

Books

BY WISDOM A HOUSE IS BUILT AND THROUGH UNDERSTANDING IT IS ESTABLISHED; THROUGH KNOWLEDGE ITS ROOMS ARE FILLED WITH RARE AND BEAUTIFUL TREASURES

(diy) Family Gallery Wall

Hanging a gallery wall is one of my favorite ways to add style and reflect who we are as a family. You can share your story through the photos you display, the artwork you choose, or a mix. There are different styles of gallery walls, but I like ones with an organic flow. This also gives us more grace to hang pictures without everything being exactly lined up.

SUPPLIES
– photos
– frames with matting if desired
– nails and hammer

INSTRUCTIONS

1. Gather the photos and wall art you want. For charm, I chose frames that go together but aren't too matchy-matchy. If clean lines are your game, choose frames that are the same color. I like to have at least three different sizes of frames in my grouping, but you could also choose all the same size frame for more of an art gallery look.

2. Choose the wall and the starting place. Hang the largest piece of art at eye level. If creating a gallery wall above a sofa or on a large wall, I hang the largest piece in the center and work my way out on either side with smaller frames. When hanging a gallery wall on a staircase, I start with my largest frame first and then work my way up the staircase.

3. Spacing determines the success of the look. Leave up to 6″ between larger frames and 2″ or 3″ between smaller ones. Practice your layout on the floor. Position the largest frame first. This helps you map the order and spacing and avoid making extra holes in the wall. Take photos so you can reference the dry run when you start the install.

4. Check the type of hanger each frame has on the back before starting. Some require a nail or screw, while others can be hung with adhesive strips. Finishing nails are great for hanging frames in most drywall. You may need to use an anchor with a screw if the drywall hole is too big or if you have plaster walls. Adhesive strips are great for securing corners of frames to the wall to prevent tilting later.

5. After hanging a few frames, take a step back to assess and adjust early. If a frame looks disconnected, move it in a little closer. It doesn't have to be perfectly symmetrical, but equal spacing will create a balanced look.

TIP

You do not need an anchor for light frames or if you find a stud. A few misses? Hide extra holes with the picture you are hanging, or a quick dab of spackle and some touch-up paint will keep your secret.

THE
DINING ROOM

{ A Place to Gather }

Welcoming friends and loved ones to gather over a meal is one of my favorite things to do (in fact, I wrote a whole book about it), but the dining room isn't all about gathering for a meal. It's the place we can come together, laugh, play board games, craft and create, and build memories from the conversations and connections formed around the table. It can become the hearth and heart of many homes.

I confess that our dining room was not the easiest room for me to restyle. You may be thinking to yourself, "How hard could it be? You have a dining room table with some chairs around it, right?" Yet the more I looked at it and asked myself, "Do I really love this space?" the more I felt like something was off. I didn't feel refreshed when I was in there.

At the time, I was starting to discover my own decor style, and most of the pieces I had didn't go with that style. By the way, let me encourage you: Your style will evolve, so don't be afraid to evolve with it. I know my own style was always with me—I just hadn't fully discovered it or figured out how to execute or communicate it.

So for a while, the dining room was merely the room we walked through to get to our living room. A room that we used only for a few occasions—exactly what I didn't intend for it to become. I was uninspired to be in that space and uninspired to remedy it. I made the best of it at the time, but once I finally got our living room to the cozy, inviting space it is today, I couldn't help but feel like my dining room was giving me the ugly stare down every time I glanced at it or passed through it. So finally, something had to be done.

As I daydreamed of my ideal dining space, I envisioned a warm and inviting setting designed for comfort so family and friends would want to stay gathered around the table long after the last bite of dessert. To keep my budget in check and me on track, I decided to focus on furniture choices, accessories that are inviting, and architectural details to create the calm and beauty that could also become sophisticated with a lit candle, special tablescape touches, or a favorite holiday meal.

The longing for that casual, light, and beautiful dining room helped me shift my current dining room decor into what I wanted it to be and not what was reflected in the trends. Ultimately, that longing is not about style, but about people and fellowship and the many gifts of gathering in a setting shaped with love and intention.

Where to Start

Identifying what you don't want can be very helpful in focusing on what you do want (and your style). I knew I would shy away from the stereotypical formal dining room style that was prevalent when I was a kid. Many of those dining rooms felt designated for special occasions and were not welcoming spaces for children. I viewed that style as untouchable and uninviting. I wanted our dining room to be as welcoming as the other rooms, offering

equal parts refreshment and elegance, with a relaxed approach, because that reflects my true style.

How would I go about shaping a room I love that has potential for game nights and gatherings? Can you relate to this hope for a room that isn't just one thing, yet has a cohesive style? Clarifying your priorities—*why* you want to make a change—will help you decide *how*.

I identified the objects in the dining room that I felt clashed or didn't go with the design aesthetic I was after and began writing a list of improvements we could make over time. Motivate yourself with simple goals and next steps. If you ever lose sight of the initial vision, this will help you get it back, and each moment of progress will give you a charge of inspiration to tackle the next one.

The Evolution of a Just-Right Look
{Furniture}

I have always loved the look and the invitation of a long farmhouse table. Thankfully, the worn look complemented the overall relaxed feel I was after. To get a good sense of what our dining room was missing, I compiled some inspiration photos of dining rooms I loved and began to take notice of the things they had in common.

All of the dining rooms with a farmhouse table also included mismatched chairs, and some of them had a bench. Some had a collection of different antique chairs, while others had a bench on one side and upholstered chairs on the other. Almost all the dining rooms showed unmatched chairs at the ends of the table. I loved this look of a pieced-together dining set. It was more casual than a traditional dining room with all matching furniture, which meant I could incorporate my own personal taste.

In my design dictionary (should I ever write one), "unmatched" pretty much means "an opportunity for creativity!" So count me in.

Our dining room furniture was initially an oval hand-me-down table and matching chairs. It was dated, so to hide its age I covered it with a white tablecloth. Then I worked up the courage to try painting it. Since this dining set was free to me and nothing fancy, I wasn't too worried if I messed it up. I figured the worst-case scenario was that I would make it uglier and then have to drape the tablecloth back over it. Nothing to lose except a little time for research and labor. To make my efforts count, I sought out advice about which paint is the best for furniture. One of the associates at our local paint store pointed me to a paint specifically for furniture that would bond to wood and have a more durable finish. I started by priming my table and chairs with Zinsser B-I-N shellac-based primer because it sticks to all surfaces, and then I used a black oil-based paint, hoping the modern finish would help give my set the updated look it needed.

I purchased two new end chairs. Since I had painted our table and chairs black, I chose wicker chairs in a pretty gray wash that would bring some needed texture to the room. Adding different end chairs immediately gave our dining room a more personal touch and exuded the style I was after.

Not too long after this, I admitted to my husband that I was still dreaming of a farm table. For some reason, we both decided we were game to try building one. Using unfinished lumber from the hardware store and table legs from an old dining table, my husband built the table and a bench. Then I got to work putting a finish on them. This project together was the turning point in our dining room style, and it showed us that when we work together and combine our skills, amazing things can happen.

Since then our dining room has evolved by incorporating different accent chairs and a new bench. Once our dining set was complete, I got the courage to sand and refinish the hand-me-down dresser we use as a buffet. The resulting lighter tone complemented the other wood tones in the space. Our dining room

TIP

A chandelier can be hung anywhere from 28 to 36 inches above the table.

transformation was a process, so we learned to make little tweaks along the way as our budget allowed. Our space evolved into what we wanted. I had a beautiful table, a bench, and chairs, and I didn't have to worry so much about dings and scratches because they would only add to the charm and character.

Adding Lightness to a Space
{Styling + Accessories}

Filling your dining room with details that inspire you will encourage your family to gather in there more often, ensuring that this space isn't destined for formal occasions only.

When my husband and I got married, black accessories were all the rage. It was the early 2000s, and every home decor store had shelves filled with black candlesticks, chunky black picture frames, and black lamps. There is nothing wrong with black accessories or furniture, but when I looked back over my inspiration photos for our dining room, the spaces I loved were filled with lighter wood tones, white accessories, and pops of greenery—none of which I had, and all of which I wanted.

I was craving a light and airy dining room with warm texture, so I incorporated accessories that were mostly white, and I added natural textures, such as wicker chairs and woven blinds. This helped me achieve the look I was after. I grabbed a can of white spray paint and began painting, turning my darker picture frames, candlesticks, and more into lovely white accents. Each time I strolled through HomeGoods, I hunted for just-right white dishes and platters. Slowly I began to swap out our old accessories for ones that aligned with my design style. I brought in white farmhouse pitchers to use as vases, and reclaimed glass jugs to use as accessories. Their smooth surface balanced the weathered wood tones in the candlesticks and pieces of driftwood I like to incorporate into my spaces. Throughout this book you will definitely see my love for the New England coastline reflected in our style. Your favorite place will tell you a lot about what nourishes you visually.

Try this out for your dining area. Find a photo of the look you love. Now stand in your dining area and note which of your accessories fit into this vision. Which ones need to be moved elsewhere or be given away? This is important because dining rooms don't typically have the multiple surface areas that a living room provides for accessory arrangements. Don't crowd your surfaces. Instead, keep items to a minimum.

One way to add to my look of lightness without adding to a surface area was to buy an actual light. Don't you love it when the answer is obvious? I decided a chandelier would elevate the space to elegant. And the style of the chandelier would also keep it in the realm of casual beauty. I chose a chandelier that had both a farmhouse style and the look of aged wood. It's the perfect statement piece, and it casts the perfect light on the cozy room.

When you are traveling or at the local flea market and are considering buying an accessory, choose one that has meaning to you, and choose objects in colors that are certain to illuminate the look you love instead of distract from it by adding clutter.

What else adds the color or composition of light or dark you are after? Curtains or rugs, like the lighting fixture choice, are elements that naturally suit a room because of their function. If you like a bold pop of color, try incorporating an area rug with a bold pattern or curtains in a fabric of fun tones or vibrant designs. If light and airy is more your thing, you might prefer neutral curtains that softly filter in natural light paired with a jute rug that is durable against spills but adds rich texture. Curtains and rugs can soften the look presented by the hard surfaces of dining room furniture.

As with furniture, so with accessories: Curate the elements over time rather than purchasing them in sets. Let each piece you

choose help you tell your story. Maybe it's incorporating a china set or serving platters you inherited from a relative or family friend. Have you collected any bottles or vases over the years that would make a pretty display in a hutch or on a buffet?

Think of bringing in pieces that not only reflect your personal style but reflect light and openness to welcome others into your ongoing story.

Bring in the Warmth
{Architectural Details}

Our dining room was the first room I painted when we moved into our house ten years ago. I picked the color months prior to moving in, and from the first brush stroke of Woodsmoke Gray, I knew this warm, medium-toned gray was the right color. The way it looked next to our crisp white, chunky trim felt like a match made in heaven. I love it when that happens.

While I focused on other areas of the home for a while, I would pause at the entrance to the dining room to take in the room as a whole. What worked? What didn't? I knew the next level of warmth and visual interest would come from adding architectural details to the walls. The first choice was a chair rail, which we installed using a level and a finish nail gun. I painted the area below the rail white. Yes, I took my chances on what my toddlers' little hands could do to a white wall. To my surprise and despite my fears, the walls stayed clean, and our dining room stayed like this for a couple years. Installing the chair rail confirmed that adding architectural details to the walls in our dining room was key to adding warmth. Like a couch with layers of soft throw pillows, a room with architectural layers, like wall moldings, will be cozy and interesting.

Sometimes a success in one category is a long-term win, but sometimes it provides inspiration to go on to the next level. This was the case with the chair rail. That one simple addition made such an impact, I knew I wanted to go further. This time we

TIP

Tablecloths don't have to be just for tables; they can make inexpensive drapes too. Hang them with clips to swap out your curtains seasonally for a fresh look.

raised the height of the wall moldings. We removed the chair rail and applied a white board-and-batten treatment to the bottom two-thirds of the wall, leaving the top third of the walls gray. The space finally extended the warm invitation I longed for. Sure, it took some explaining to my husband why we were removing the chair rail I liked in order to put up new moldings. (Hmm . . . I did the same thing with the furniture evolution. Notice a trend?) But the first round of improvement wasn't a mistake. It gave me the confidence I needed and the real-life research to know wainscoting would add substantial and satisfying warmth.

The Family-Friendly Dining Room

I will always want dining furniture that is pretty enough for entertaining and durable enough for everyday meals and craft times. This allows me to focus on what really matters—my family gathered around our table.

The durable table choice was already made—literally—so next up were chairs. I chose slipcovered parsons chairs to flank the side of the table opposite a bench. They provided a comfortable place to sit and easy cleanup. If a craft time or dinner is exceptionally messy, I have our kids sit on the wooden bench so it can be quickly wiped clean.

I loved the look of the Pottery Barn slipcover dining chairs, but I couldn't afford them. So I searched for an option that looked similar to my inspiration and would fit my budget. I found the best bang for my buck at IKEA. I could find parson dining chairs online at most retailers, but finding a style that came with a removable slipcover was a little more challenging. I watched tutorials on making slipcovers out of painter's drop cloths, but IKEA gave the option for purchasing a cotton slipcover that fit the chair perfectly, making the overall chair and slipcover cost less than anywhere else. I was thrilled to find the look I wanted for so much less, and I didn't have to try out my beginner sewing skills.

BRE'S TOP 10
ESSENTIALS

Wood table

Statement chandelier

Sideboard or buffet

Comfortable seating

Candlesticks and
candles

Interesting wall decor

Everyday centerpiece

Table linens

Floor-length curtains

Mirror

Family-friendly options nicely translate into guest-friendly options. Our slipcovered side chairs allow our guests to take a deep breath, not fretting over an accidental spill, leaving everyone feeling relaxed for conversation and fellowship around the table.

As my dining space has transformed, I am no longer the only one who cares about how it looks and feels and what it provides. I've seen my kids being eager to set the table or help clear dishes away. See? Miracles happen. This tells me they too enjoy sharing a meal and gathering together—a truth that is a far greater blessing than any of the things I have in that space.

diy Farmhouse Dining Table

Building your own farmhouse table is more doable than you think. Thanks to the simple designs and the variety of styles, the option to find or make a table that suits your style are endless. I shared earlier how making our own farmhouse table was the most affordable option for us. I have to admit that it was also my favorite option. I look at that table daily and am filled with a sense of appreciation for its uniqueness and the story of partnering with my husband to create it for each other and for our family and guests. Listed below is a tutorial to make your very own farmhouse table . . . and some special memories too.

SUPPLIES
- 4 dining table legs
- 6) 1" x 8" x 6' boards
- 2) 1" x 4" x 10' boards
- Kreg Jig
- 1½" pocket hole screws
- wood glue
- Weathered Wood Restoration stain
- Minwax Driftwood stain
- Finish: Miss Mustard Seed White Wax

1. Cut two 1 x 4s to 67" lengths, and two 1 x 4s to 24" lengths. This will be your table apron and what you will attach your legs to. On the same side of the cut 1 x 4s, drill 1½" pocket holes every 10" facing upward, and two pocket holes on either end of the 1 x 4 facing outward. Be sure to have all pocket holes facing upward when attaching the legs to the apron.

2. Attach the legs to the apron using the 1½" pocket hole screws and wood glue.

3. Cut four 1 x 4s to 12" lengths, with 45-degree angles on opposite ends. Drill two pocket holes on both ends of these 12" pieces on the longer, non-angled side. Attach the 12" pieces to the inside of all four corners of the apron using wood glue and 1½" pocket hole screws.

4. To build the tabletop, cut five 1 x 8s to 69" lengths. Drill 1½" pocket holes about 8" apart on the underside of these pieces, and attach the boards together using 1½" pocket hole screws and wood glue.

5. To attach the breadboard ends, measure and cut the remaining 1 x 8s to the width of your tabletop, as measurements could vary depending on widths of tabletop boards. Attach them to the tabletop using 1½" pocket hole screws and wood glue. (Breadboard ends are the two planks on the ends of the tabletop that run perpendicular to the main table boards.)

6. Flip the tabletop over so all the pocket holes are facing upward. Center the table base on the tabletop and square it up. Starting at the center of the end aprons, attach through the predrilled pocket holes from step 1 with 1½" pocket hole screws. Work your way outward, and then continue on the side aprons.

7. Flip the table over and stain using two coats of Weathered Wood Restoration stain, followed by one coat of Minwax Driftwood stain. Finish with Miss Mustard Seed White Wax.

THE
KITCHEN

{ A Place to Nourish }

When we spend time in the kitchen, we offer our families the gift of nourishment. That gift is served not only through the food we prepare but also the warm welcome and memories we share there. I remember spending time in the kitchen with my mom, catching up after school and filling her in on my day as she prepared dinner for our family. We had an eat-in kitchen, so much of my time was spent at our table doing homework or another activity, talking, and eating my favorite snack—cinnamon toast with lots of butter.

Those sweet memories fueled my desire to have a kitchen with a long island where my kids can have a snack and do a craft or homework while I am cooking or putting away groceries. Today, our kitchen island is the hub where my family gathers and connects over breakfast or reunites for dinner at day's end. Everyday life happens here. I want it to be special and functional for all these reasons.

Over the years we've rented apartments with awkward or tiny kitchens. Even this one was not set up ideally when we moved in. There was no money in the budget for major renovations, so I fixed my sights on the cosmetic changes I could make in the meantime. Those past and present scenarios taught me how to turn just about any kitchen into a space that I love, even if it isn't a Pinterest dream kitchen.

I brightened it up with a fresh coat of light gray paint (Gray Owl by Benjamin Moore), covering the blah tan, coffee color that had kept the space dark and gloomy. This brought out the cheerier tones in the counters too. Next I brought in lighter accessories piece by piece. I continued making little changes along the way to transform it into the farmhouse kitchen I was dreaming of.

Having a good design in a kitchen doesn't require us to gut the existing one. Often that's not an option due to space, time, or finances. I believe in the power of making tiny improvements over time to transform our humble kitchens into spaces that offer us nourishment and contentment. My initial go-to design elements include accessories and styling, lighting, and architectural details.

Kitchens can be the most difficult to envision "decorating" because they are so functional. If you don't have fancy new appliances and your cabinets leave you discouraged, don't lose hope. Or perhaps you have a new kitchen, but it doesn't reflect your personal style. You can still find your way to loving the space. I have yet to build a dream kitchen from scratch, but I have figured out a thing or two about decorating a kitchen that will inspire you to try new recipes and that puts a smile on your face as it welcomes you in each morning to start your day.

FARMHOUSE {EST. 1841}

favourite
RECIPE

today's
SPECIALS

PEOPLE WHO
LOVE to EAT
are always
THE
BEST
People"

~Julia Child

Where to Start

Tell me about your kitchen. Are you inspired to tackle that fancy new recipe or sit with a cup of tea and happily craft your grocery list? Or do you feel like leaving as soon as you whip up a meal?

This is your starting place for creating a space that inspires baking and laughing, making memories with family, and enjoying coffee and life chats with friends. Focus on the things you can change. And then look forward with joy to the ways you can continue making it a better reflection of you.

All the changes I made happened over time, so be encouraged. I had to wait on some things, like nicer accessories and floors, yet the transformation was still moving in a good direction. If you are willing to put in the time, you can end up with a room that you love—without breaking the bank!

Grab a notebook and brainstorm ideas to improve what you have. Is your starter goal to refresh the room with new paint? Or to remove a cupboard door so you have a unit of open shelves? You are getting in the zone! So fill your favorite mug (because we all have one) with something yummy to drink, and let's get started.

Serve Up Beauty with Functional Items
{Accessories + Styling}

In a kitchen, organization and decor go hand in hand for a look that's put together and beautiful. The biggest lesson I've learned when it comes to adding decor to your kitchen is that it cannot be in the way. Sure, beautiful bowls displayed on your countertop are nice to look at, but if you have to keep moving those bowls out of the way because you need more work surface for preparing food, then they have become a nuisance.

I learned early on that incorporating pieces or features that look pretty and serve a purpose is a win-win. Displaying items you've collected or inherited is one way you can tell your story through your decor. Perhaps it's a stack of antique linens you found at a yard sale that remind you of a relative. Tuck them neatly in a basket to incorporate some softness to your display. A display of antique cutting boards becomes unexpected artwork and also showcases what interests you.

Sure, I could use a plain old plastic platter to serve dinner. Or for a few dollars more, I could buy the beautiful serving platter that stops me in my tracks when I'm walking down the store aisle. It makes a better presentation for my meal, and when I'm not using it, I can display it on a shelf or backsplash and add some decor to my kitchen as well. The open shelves in our kitchen are a perfect example of this.

We don't have a pantry and are super tight on storage, but I couldn't bear to see my favorite white cake stands and other white serveware stored in boxes in our basement. So we utilized an empty wall in our kitchen by installing floating shelves. Every item was carefully chosen to match the look and style I wanted for our kitchen. We store baking ingredients in large glass canisters that resemble old apothecary jars found in country stores. Our cow creamer and batter bowl reflect our love for farmhouse breakfasts and get used on the weekends. Even the dog's food is neatly stored in a white enamel trashcan so it can be out in plain sight and blend in with the decor in our kitchen.

These items look like they are on display, but we use them every day. Function and beauty can be paired perfectly. When you look around your kitchen for areas to style, think of decorative storage containers and ways to display your everyday items. If you have beautiful plates, don't hide them behind closed cabinet doors—display them to add beautiful decor to your kitchen. This becomes a wonderful way to visually nourish yourself and your family.

Let Your Style Shine

{Lighting}

Did you know that while lighting casts its glow and helps us with tasks, it also acts as decor? Don't you love it when that happens? The design and finish of a fixture adds style, especially to rooms where other decor might be at a minimum. Your priority is to illuminate the spaces you are working in. If you can add or replace lighting, consider the key places: Over the cooktop and prep areas are among the most important. Overhead lighting in a kitchen doesn't have to be an afterthought. This should be a place where you let your true design style shine.

When we first moved into this home, the lighting in our kitchen was small and builder basic and resembled track lighting. It definitely wasn't my style. When the light over my sink burned out, I jumped at the chance to swap out that one and the light over our island. I searched for something that fit my decor style better. I knew I wouldn't have a chance to replace it again for years, so I wanted it to count toward adding to the mood of the room and the overall look of our home. Because our house was built in 1846 and resembles a true New England farmhouse, I chose barn light pendants that perfectly complemented our farmhouse style.

Consider your personal lighting needs. Do you want bright ambient lighting, commonly provided by overhead pendants and chandeliers? Perhaps you don't have an island but still want to add in some character with lighting fixtures. There are many flush-mount lighting options now in a variety of different styles. Some of my favorite places to look are Overstock, Amazon, and Lowe's. Or perhaps you need more task lighting. Wall sconces are a great way to add a little bit of fun personality while offering concentrated light on a particular area. Don't forget about under-cabinet lights! They offer a great illumination for countertop work spaces and provide a soft glow when left on at night. You can choose

HOW TO STYLE YOUR KITCHEN'S OPEN SHELVES

❶ Visualize an X over the shelves. Starting with the top and bottom corners, place your taller items there. I place my glass canisters on the bottom shelf to the right, and I use my cake stand collection to fill in the other corners. **TIP:** I keep heavier items on the bottom shelf to avoid having to reach overhead for them.

❷ Where my X intersects on the middle shelf, I hung a piece of artwork. This creates a focal point and grounds the entire display. You could use a breadboard or an antique platter.

❸ Group like items together—a set of drinking glasses, plates in the same color, or nested mixing bowls. This creates a cohesive look. Place them diagonally from each other for a symmetrical look. For example, I have a grouping of cake stands on the top left corner, and then a second set of cake stands diagonally across on the middle shelf on the right side.

❹ Add in height. Use similar pieces in different heights, or stack items on top of other larger pieces to create more height if your shelving clearance allows. I like to tuck in little bowls and measuring cups on some stacked pieces for more height and interest.

❺ Bring in the green. To finish off my open shelves, I always like to add in a little green, whether it's some flowers or a plant. That pop of green adds a different texture to my display and really brings the whole thing to life.

from hardwired, battery operated, or rechargeable under-cabinet lighting to fit your specific needs.

Not long ago, I added a table lamp to a small dresser in our kitchen. It was a gloomy day, and I was desperate for more light. I brought in one of the table lamps from our living room and plugged it in. Voila! Instantly our kitchen felt warm, cozy, and a bit brighter too. If adding additional overhead lights isn't an option, think outside the box. I love that my new lamp offers my kitchen the same cozy effect I get in my living room. Who knows . . . this just might become a kitchen design staple for you too.

Transform Trouble Areas
{Architectural Details}

One ugly wall in our kitchen glared at me and taunted me with an evil wall laugh because every time I considered how to improve it, the task felt hopeless. Perhaps you have an area like this in your home too—a space that you can't imagine how to restyle.

I referred to my trouble spot as the "wall of doors." It had three doors with a tiny portion of wall between two of the doors. I used to sit at my island and just stare at it, trying to figure out some way to improve this visual catastrophe. Each of the doors leads somewhere, so removing them wasn't an option. Whenever we've made improvements to our house, I've tried to keep the integrity of the farmhouse's original character and structure in mind. Since I couldn't physically move the doors, the next option was to somehow visually connect them so the wall felt cohesive. The tiny portion of wall that was between two of the doors didn't have the depth for a piece of furniture or cabinets. And to add to the dilemma, the end of our island was too close to place anything on that wall that extended out.

I gave this much thought. I was reminded of the older country kitchens, where plates were displayed on the wall on peg boards and different racks. After seeing a plate rack wall in my good

friend KariAnne's kitchen, I had all the ammo I needed to make a choice.

We gathered our materials and built a recessed plate rack, where I could display serving platters and cutting boards. Now the space between two of the doors had purpose. The plate rack wall added a focal point to our kitchen, and it took the attention away from the odd vignette of three doors on one wall.

Once the plate rack wall was installed, I didn't stop there. (If you follow my blog, you probably guessed this!) I had some design momentum, so I thought about other ways I could make the kitchen homier and more appealing. I have always loved the look of sliding barn doors. They are full of farmhouse charm and so functional without requiring much space. I knew this would be the perfect addition for character, style, and warmth. We installed a sliding barn door directly next to the plate rack wall, allowing us to swap out the door in the middle that leads to our basement for one that adds charm to the overall look and feel of the space. Our farmhouse kitchen felt complete with the architectural details of the barn door and plate rack wall. The "wall of doors" might still be there in essence, but now it's a wall that adds interest and character to our kitchen. A once hopeless and terribly annoying part of the room now offers inspiration and delight back into the space.

The Family-Friendly Kitchen

Whether a kitchen is the place to congregate or the room to pass through on the way to other spaces, you need a plan, or things will get cluttered quickly.

When we lived in an apartment, I had a kitchen cart that served as an island. When we moved into our present home, we finally had a real island. But instead of parting with the cart, I used it for additional surface area by the door. The purpose was ill-defined, so as humans do, we started to fill it with everything—books, grocery totes, bags, mittens, and more. Since we use the kitchen

TIP

When hanging pendant lights over an island, keep 30 to 32 inches between the countertop and the bottom of the pendant.

entrance as our main one, we also had growing piles of shoes and stools that had morphed into casual coat racks.

Finally, I hit my limit. No doubt it was a day I tripped over snow boots. I loved the cart and had saved money to purchase it, but it had to go. In this home and with my family's routine, it had triggered more clutter, not less. I sold it to a friend and started to brainstorm solutions to our lack of a mudroom.

I needed our shoe storage to be practical and not intrusive. I placed a narrow bench below the windows and tucked crates underneath to hold our shoes. This provided both a place to take off our shoes and store them out of sight. I purchased items that reinforced our decor. The simple farmhouse-style bench was just right for toddlers to perch on while I helped them tie their shoes, and the antique wooden crates placed underneath were charming. Storage that's not only functional but contributes to the decor is always a win-win.

Maybe you don't need shoe storage in your kitchen, but are there other areas that you wish served your family better? I have been known to rearrange my cabinets to keep the kids' most-used items all in easy-to-reach spots.

Setting up your kitchen in a way that serves your family's needs and draws them into the space ensures you all receive the nourishment your home is meant to provide.

BRE'S TOP 10
ESSENTIALS

Cake stands

Tea towels

White plates

Ceramic creamers

Antique silverware

Glass canisters

Cutting boards

Batter bowls

Plants

Crock to hold
cooking utensils

diy Plate Rack

We recessed our plate rack wall between two door frames. Instead of recessing it, you might have enough space to mount this design directly to the wall, securing it to a stud or using anchors to secure it to the wall. The size of your plate rack wall will determine how much wood you need to build it. I have included our dimensions below for reference.

SUPPLIES
- 1" x 2" pine boards (count depends on how big you want the plate rack)
- ½" x ¾" pine screen molding
- ¼" x ¾" rounded edge pine screen molding
- (1) 4' x 8' sheet of ¾" MDF primed beadboard panel, cut to desired size

PLATE RACK DIMENSIONS
- 73" x 38"

CUT LIST
- (2) 1 x 2s cut to 73" boards
- (5) 1 x 2s cut to 37" boards
- (4) ½ x ¾ pine screen molding cut to 38"
- (4) ¼ x ¾ rounded edge pine screen molding cut to 38"

INSTRUCTIONS

1. Assemble the frame using a finish nail gun to attach the two 1 x 2 x 73" pine boards to two of the 1 x 2 x 37" boards, creating a rectangle.

2. Attach the primed beadboard for the backing of your plate rack wall.

3. If you are attaching the plate rack directly to the wall, determine the desired shelf height, but do not attach the shelves yet. Screw the plate rack to the wall where the shelf placement will be so that the shelves will eventually cover your holes. If you are recessing the plate rack between door frames, drill in the screws on the sides of the frame where the shelves will be so they will eventually cover the holes.

4. Install the other three 1 x 2 x 37" boards for the shelves. This will be the base for your shelf.

5. Once the 1 x 2 shelves are in place, attach the ¼ x ¾ rounded edge screen molding, cut to the entire width, with the rounded edge facing up toward the 1 x 2 shelves. This will create a lip so your plates don't slide out the bottom.

6. Attach the ¼ x ¾ screen molding, cut to the entire width, three inches above the rounded edge molding to keep the plates securely on the shelf.

7. Finish with caulk or paintable silicone to fill in any gaps. Paint the color of your choice.

THE BEDROOM
AND BATHROOM

{ Places to Refresh }

In many homes, the bedroom gets tended to last . . . if at all. And bathrooms get cleaned to be presentable to the public but are often last in the decor-improvement lineup. In this chapter, we'll focus on how to make your bedroom a retreat and turn a bathroom of any size into a place for relaxation and refreshment.

When I was young, my bedroom was my space to express a budding interest in creating beautiful surroundings. I could rearrange my furniture whenever I wanted to, however I wanted to, and believe me, I did! Those early years shaped my desire to make my bedroom a special place in every home I've lived in.

When my husband and I moved into a new apartment as a married couple, we were exhausted from packing, loading, and unloading, and a bit cranky and sore from lifting heavy boxes and furniture. As our moving day came to an end, my husband decided to return to the old apartment for one last walk through. After he left, I looked around our new space and at the towers of boxes, wondering where to begin.

My first thought was "I don't want to unpack...I just want to rest!"

Then the lightbulb turned on. I would surprise my husband by setting up our bedroom while he was gone. I couldn't think of anything better than having a sanctuary ready for rest and recovery. (And a place to hide from all the boxes.)

I got to work quickly setting up our bedroom. Thanks to a skill I learned from all those years of redecorating my room as a kid, I could move most of the furniture by myself, sliding it on bath towels across the hardwood floors. I made the bed with fresh linens, hung our curtains, put away clothes, and propped a mirror above one of the dressers, all before he got home.

You can imagine his surprise when I opened the bedroom door and revealed a cozy space just beyond all the boxes. The relief and gratitude I saw on his face confirmed that having a soft place to land at the end of that day—and every day—was what we both longed for.

Now in our bedroom, you can find me trying out new paint colors as the mood strikes. After I shifted my color palette from a restful blue to a serene white, I turned my focus toward architectural details, layers and textures, and lighting. I knew these enhancements would welcome us to transition from busy days to restful nights.

Prepare a bedroom and bathroom that bless you with the gift of refreshment. I'll share bathroom decor ideas at the end of this chapter. Right now, let's look at some simple changes that will turn your bedroom into a haven.

Where to Start

When I was a kid, instead of taking notes in school, I drew floor plans and new furniture arrangements for my bedroom. I loved trying different configurations, much to the dismay of my sister who, for a time, shared a room with me but did not share my desire to shake things up. I invite you to experience a bedroom refresh by moving a few pieces around. If space allows, move your bed to a different wall. Change the location of your dresser. Or swap

you will
never regret
having
hope.

your nightstands for a different side table or a small dresser you already have. Take a look at the result. Did a once-congested corner open so you have room for a chair that's perfect for morning coffee and quiet time?

Now decide how you want the space to feel. Much of my bedroom's decor is inspired by stays at places that offered the ultimate in comfort and serenity. Have you stayed somewhere that could inspire your bedroom refresh? Which design elements offered the most refreshment and evoked the feel you want? The plush layers of bedding? The calming choice of color? You are on your way to a bedroom that will be a gift to you (and your spouse, if married).

Surrounded by Cozy Additions
{Architectural Details}

Our bedroom felt flat. The walls lacked interest despite the few pieces of artwork and pictures I displayed. I knew we needed the character that architectural details provide.

I had come across the board-and-batten wall treatment while flipping through a magazine. It stopped me dead in my tracks, and as I studied this magazine page, I knew it would look perfect in our bedroom. We first added it as an accent wall behind our bed. Once we installed it, I was struck by how it created the same serenity found at the charming inns New England is known for. I bet you can guess what happened next. Sooner than later we ended up installing it on the rest of the walls as well. Aaahhh.

Now that I was motivated by this country inn ambience, I decided to soften the look of the room by switching over to mostly white bedding, which I will talk about more in the next section. In decorating with mostly white, I have learned that the more texture you can add to a space, the less stark it will feel. Our bedroom was the only room in our house that had a popcorn ceiling. I wanted to remedy that and add architectural interest at the same time, so I added DIY shiplap planks to our ceiling. If you've frequented Pinterest anytime

TIP

Hang hats on the wall as artwork to showcase your personal style.

in the past five years, it's safe to say you've seen some form of shiplap applied to walls. It can also be a great way to cover up or add interest to a ceiling. Using quarter-inch underlayment plywood, ripped down (cut along the grain) into five-inch planks, I was able to use our finish nail gun and attach the planks to our ceiling in one afternoon. I chose to paint the planks white and used a nickel-sized gap between each board to provide enough texture to offset all the white.

I was delighted by the style strides I had made with architectural touches. I would walk by the bedroom during the day just to take in the simple beauty and get a dose of cozy. These two additions took some planning and labor, but they were overall inexpensive choices that added great value in the form of warm details and character. They changed our master bedroom into a sanctuary that nourished us at the end of each day. Honestly, there isn't one evening since these projects have been completed when I haven't entered our bedroom with gratitude for the chance to create a place for rest that welcomes us after the crazy days, the ho-hum days, and the many days in between.

Linens and Layers for Comfort
{Texture + Layers}

Creating a room that feels like a refuge is an intentional act of bringing peace into the space. I can't wait to jump in our bed after it has been layered with rows of plush pillows. It calls out to me, saying "Dive on in and stay awhile." Apparently my kiddos hear the same message, because they also jump headfirst into the plush landing every chance they get.

Is your bed crying for attention rather than whispering a welcome to you at the end of the day? It could be time to bring on the layers of love. Nothing says comfort and indulgence to me like layers of soft down comforters and quilted blankets.

Over the years, I have swapped our bedding over to a mostly white palette. I love the all-white bedding in hotels or inns, but it

took me some time to get it right. More blankets won't always mean more comfort. When I started adding in layers of different kinds of bedding with different textures and patterns, it all came together.

My base was created with sheets of silky sateen. I then added a crisp cotton pick-stitch quilt and a soft linen duvet cover. These are all white, but each piece adds a slightly different tone and texture for a casual yet refined look. While linen can be expensive, it has a worn-in feel, which keeps things relaxed. I always keep my eyes peeled for it when I'm strolling through stores. Think about fabrics you love. You might prefer jersey knit or flannel sheets for your base and chunkier blankets for another layer.

For my lush layers, I gravitate toward natural fibers, like cotton, linen, and down, because they are breathable and feel good against the skin. Yes, I am totally that person who walks down the bedding aisle and touches everything. By the way, the best time to shop for bedding is in the beginning of a new year.

Don't forget about window treatments, which are often overlooked, for their potential to improve the mood and feel of a space. They are actually one of the easiest and best options for adding rich layers to your refuge. Curtain panels layered over bamboo blinds introduce a warm, woven texture and visual interest.

Notice how much sunlight pours in throughout the day to determine which window treatments serve your quest for beauty and function. If your room is flooded with sunlight in the early morning hours, consider blackout curtains to keep the sunlight to a minimum—allowing for a deeper, longer sleep. If you have a dark bedroom, consider sheer fabrics and adjustable blinds.

Aglow with Ambience
{Lighting}

Lighting in a bedroom can be a design element that highlights your personality and creates ambience. We've probably all lived with the standard, not-so-pretty light fixture that adorns the majority of bedroom ceilings, but you can now cast your bedroom in lovely light.

Define what your lighting wants and needs are. I love the look of a beautiful chandelier hanging over a bed, but the ceiling height in our bedroom just doesn't allow for a light fixture of that style. When I was in high school, my bedroom had a ceiling fan and light combo. Unfortunately, the unit was too big for my small bedroom. It hung down so low that I hit my arms on it every time I got dressed. So, word to the wise: When selecting a primary fixture, keep in mind the ceiling height, how much natural light the windows provide, the secondary lighting you will have, and your overall lighting needs. And regardless of whether your central light has a fan, choose one in a finish that will complement your overall bedroom style or pop as a statement piece.

Once you have established your main overhead lighting, add complementary lighting to your nightstands or bedside tables. This is a key place where form meets function. Choosing a table lamp that reflects your style is an enjoyable way to create ambient light for reading at night or a relaxing glow before bedtime. I tend to keep the rest of the decor in my bedroom to a minimum, so table lamps offer me a chance to add some personality and interest without my nightstands becoming cluttered by accessories.

Think of your favorite outfit accessories. Do you tend toward an elegant look? A lamp with a shiny metal or crystal base is a great way to glam up your space. If you like a more industrial look, shop for task desk lamps. If space is limited, do not fear. Adding sconces to the walls on either side of the bed is another way to create task and mood lighting without taking up surface space. Many sconces come with the option of being either hardwired or plugged in, so be sure to check the specs before buying.

We swapped out our standard lighting for a flush-mount ceiling light that added texture and complemented the decor I longed for. The beaded ceiling light adds a touch of whimsy, while the raw finish of the wooden beads speaks to my love of weathered wood. My husband loves the functionality of the ceiling light, but I'm drawn to the soft ambient lighting from the bedside lamps. One

of my favorite home rituals is to go to the bedroom when the sun starts to set and turn on our bedside lamps. When we return later to ease into our bedtime routine, the cozy glow welcomes our weary selves.

The Family-Friendly Bedroom and Bath

I hate putting away laundry. My piles of clean laundry are stacked around our bedroom and prevent it from becoming a restful retreat. Maybe you are familiar with this clutter scenario in your bedroom or bathroom. Are scattered toiletries, towels, and clothing keeping you from refreshment? You will feel better when everything is in its place. No math is required to love this formula:

an uncluttered space = an uncluttered mind

The objects you bring in, keep, pile up, and stash in your home will impact the ambience and your peace. You can have the prettiest bed linens, but if you have to plow through stuff to find your pillow, you've lost the benefit of those good intentions.

Every year my husband and I go through our clothes and eliminate what isn't being used. We ask, "Have I worn this in the last year?" If the answer is no, then we ask ourselves why and whether it's worth keeping. Nothing makes me happier than opening our tidy, simplified closet after the purge process. Include your kids in this annual event. Motivate them with a hearty Saturday breakfast of pancakes.

For your bathroom, private or shared, look for the right storage piece. We had no space for a double vanity, so I purchased a dresser to house toiletries and essentials. It was new but had vintage charm with antique-styled legs and a weathered wood finish. Along with the wood beam, the reclaimed wooden shelves, and the woven Roman shade, it balanced out the white tones and immediately provided the peace of organization.

After the DIY, I share a special mini-tour of the design elements and decor choices in our bathroom so you can sample a few more ideas for your own refreshing escape.

Down comforter + duvet

Area rug

Accent pillows

Layered window treatments

Bedside lamps

Accent chair or bench

Personal artwork

Cotton or linen bed skirt

Plant

Mirror

BRE'S TOP 10 ESSENTIALS

diy Board-and-Batten Accent Wall

This wainscoting wall treatment adds loads of texture. The type of walls you have may determine the type of treatment you install. If you have textured walls, you can choose to leave them textured, skim a thin layer of drywall mud over the portion of the walls where the board-and-batten will be, or use thin layers of underlayment plywood to cover the walls. In our case, since our walls are sheetrock and already smooth, we only needed to purchase the boards for this treatment. We opted for the most budget-friendly option (pine boards), but other board options include MDF, oak, or prime select, which will have no knots. Whichever option you choose, you will love the style and architectural detail this adds to your room. Let's get started.

SUPPLIES

- Boards for the base (if your trim has a beveled edge), cap, verticals, and ledge. We used 1" x 5" pine for the top boards and 1" x 3" pine for the vertical boards.
- Table saw
- Construction adhesive
- Nail gun
- Nails
- Level
- Caulk and caulking gun
- Surfacing paste (we used spackle) and sandpaper
- Primer, paint, and paint roller

INSTRUCTIONS

1. Measure your wall and determine how far apart you want your vertical boards spaced. Cut and install the baseboard and cap (the bottom and top horizontal boards).

2. Next, install the vertical boards and molding. Ensure all of the boards are level as you install them. Use construction adhesive to glue pieces to the walls. Secure the boards with nails as you work, using a nail gun. If desired, attach a ledge piece atop the cap board. Use a nail gun to secure it in place.

3. Caulk all the seams. Spackle the nail holes and sand them smooth.

4. Prime the walls and boards. When the primer is dry, paint the upper walls your desired color and paint the lower walls and boards white. Let dry.

Bathroom Highlights

Creating a bathroom you love doesn't necessarily require a full renovation or even installing new tile. No, you can refresh your bathroom and create your own spa-like retreat without swinging a sledgehammer at your walls or ripping out your bathtub.

Over the years we've done it all—applying a fresh coat of paint, adding a beadboard wallpaper treatment because we couldn't afford the real deal, or tackling a bathroom demo. It doesn't take much to make a big impact. Since bathrooms are usually the smallest rooms in the home, the tiniest details can go a long way in giving us a bathroom we can love now. Personal style comes across in everything, including mirrors, hardware, and lighting. Layering in pretty textiles, like bathmats, towels, and shower curtains, will add beauty with ease.

What would you like to change? A new shower curtain or bathmat? Are you ready to try a bolder color choice? Why not add wallpaper, paint an accent wall, or swap out your light fixture? Review your wish list, and then gather inspiration photos of bathrooms you love. That way, when you begin your project—even a cleaning or organizational endeavor—you will have a clear vision of where you want to end up. For our space, I focused on accessories and styling, architectural details, and lighting. Making a small step today can make a big change in the way you feel about the space.

Decor and More for Small Spaces
{Accessories + Styling}

Adding accessories that complement the design style you love gives a personal touch and tells a part of your story (even in a bathroom). If you love French country decor, adding square soap blocks not only feels purposeful but speaks your love language. If you like the cottage feel, a chippy white-framed mirror over your vanity is a happy thing.

When accessorizing my bathrooms, I look for pieces that I'd want in any room. I like to store Q-Tips and cotton balls in glass containers and decorative jars. Beautiful containers become functional decor. I like to channel my inner "spa getaway" when decorating, so I display candles and rolled-up white hand towels stacked in a pyramid on open shelves. Decorative soaps displayed in a glass canister, bath salts in old apothecary jars, and artwork help elevate the room's decor. I also tuck in a few small potted plants to add cheer and color.

Don't forget the accessories of scent and sound! A nice scented soap or hand lotion is always lovely. And portable speakers will immerse you, your family, or guests in soothing sounds.

Create the Cozy Factor
{Architectural Details}

We waited eight years before renovating our master bathroom upstairs, so when the time finally came, you better believe I factored in adding architectural details to the budget. In fact, that was where I started!

We have a quirky, old-house bathroom with awkward bump-outs and sloped ceilings. Instead of viewing those as obstacles, we highlighted them for character. We installed subway tile on the floors and halfway up on the walls to where the slanted ceiling started. For bonus charm, we installed tongue-and-groove planks to cover the entire ceiling. Best choice ever for a cozy cottage feel. Then we installed an old beam at the center peak of the ceiling, drawing the gaze up and adding warmth.

Walls—sloped or straight—allow for functional add-ons, such as towel racks or floating shelves. We replaced wire shelving with reclaimed wood open shelves for decorative storage, and it made a great difference. Consider beadboard, wainscoting, or shiplap when you want to turn a so-so space into an interesting one. Tile on the floor or walls will create a spa feel.

Want to do something today to add architectural interest? Shop for antique window frames or shutters, or choose architectural salvage, like corbels or gables, to use for art.

Rise and Shine
{Lighting}

The bathroom is usually the first place we step into after we awaken and our retreat later for a soaking bath or a moment of solitary quiet during a busy day. Lighting can create the "relaxing spa" mood so many of us long for.

If your bathroom has windows, you might not need task or accent lighting like we did. But if your bathroom is lacking in natural light, get creative. Sometimes just changing the lightbulb wattage will enhance the feel.

When we were ready to remodel our master bathroom, I wanted to incorporate fixtures that would make a statement. I selected sconce lights for either side of the dresser to anchor that piece, reinforce the "vanity" purpose of the dresser, and cast great light. (They are my favorite lights in the whole bathroom, but don't tell the others.)

My second-favorite is probably the vanity light above the sink. The aged brass and gooseneck arm I chose has a vintage look, and the downward-facing shade cascades plenty of functional light. Simply swap out old light fixtures, and you'll instantly refresh the space. Lamps and under-cabinet lighting also add beautiful and adjustable brightness. If you have dark corners or a dark closet, add some battery-operated lights to help you see better.

Sometimes the only thing keeping us from loving our bathroom is a simple refresh of an accessory or two. Consider one simple addition or change you can make to your bathroom right now.

BRE'S TOP 10
ESSENTIALS

White towels   Drawer organizers

Hooks   Plants

Baskets   Bath salts

Lidded jars   Framed mirror

Apothecary jars   Step stool

Reclaimed Wood Shelves

One of the areas in our home I couldn't wait to DIY is an alcove beside the shower in our master bathroom. The previous owners had installed white wire shelving, and while I tried my best to keep it organized by placing baskets on each of the shelves, it just wasn't a sufficient storage solution. Since there was no door and no room to install a door, keeping these exposed shelves looking tidy was a must. We reconfigured the alcove with wood shelves and room for lidded baskets to be stacked underneath, which helped to keep bulkier items tucked out of sight.

You can install these shelves in any type of closet or alcove with reclaimed wood or lumber from the hardware store. Whether you choose to paint or stain the wood is up to you, but the solution offers a way to refresh the white wire shelves you see in many closets today. To get started, measure the width of the space so you know how much wood you need.

SUPPLIES

- Barn wood boards. If you do not have access to barn wood, 1" x 12" boards will work just fine (the length depends on the width of your space).
- (2) 2" x 3" x 8' boards
- Standard drywall screws 1⅝" long by ½" diameter (each holds up to 75 pounds!)
- Chop saw
- Screwdriver / drill
- Level
- Measuring tape
- Sandpaper, medium grit
- Stain or paint (if using new wood)

INSTRUCTIONS

1. Measure the wall height to determine where you want your shelves to be.

2. Cut the 2 x 3 boards to 1' length (or the exact depth of your shelves boards) to create shelf brackets. Then cut 45-degree angles on one end of each board. This gives the 2 x 3s an angled end for a more finished look.

3. Use the drywall screws and a level to attach the brackets to the wall.

4. Cut barn boards or 1 x 12 boards to the length of the wall space and place them on top of the brackets. If you're using new wood, stain or paint the boards before placing them on the brackets.

5. Screw the shelf boards into the brackets.

6. You're ready to style them!

THE
UTILITY SPACE

{ A Place to Serve }

re utility spaces on your list of rooms to decorate? No? Then maybe I can change your mind, because nothing makes me want to serve my family more than when I can do it from a cheery space. I call the task areas the unsung heroes of the home—the mudroom, pantry, and laundry room, to name a few. And while every home's utility spaces look different, they all provide us with the same potential to serve . . . and to serve in style.

Doing laundry not only provides clean clothes but also shows each family member they are cared for. I actually love doing laundry. (It's the putting away clean clothes that makes me weary.) I find it to be very soothing no matter how many loads are piled in front of me. I don't have to be in the laundry room all the time, thanks to a great washer and dryer that can accommodate big loads, but I am there enough to care about how it feels.

When we love the spaces we live in, we will love working in those spaces. Our environments can dictate our moods, and I don't know about you, but I'm always looking for ways to improve my mood when I'm doing chores. In the past I focused on keeping our laundry room stocked with the essentials needed for cleaning our clothes. But as our family grew and the dirty laundry with it, I found that I enjoyed doing this mundane chore much more in a room that was also enjoyable.

Once our laundry area felt fresh and updated, I found my mood was uplifted. This helped to shift my perspective from "I'm just doing another chore" to "I'm expressing love to my family through this faithful action."

This truth sank in when I broke my foot and had to hobble around in a boot and on crutches for six weeks. Maneuvering through the house was difficult in some areas and impossible in others. I couldn't do all the usual service tasks. At first, it was a nice retreat from chores. I rested on our couch with my foot propped up on pillows and anticipated a bit of a staycation . . . if I could be patient with my temporary limits. But after a few weeks I was longing to be back on my feet again and taking care of my family. Not being able to do laundry has a funny way of giving you a fresh perspective on mundane chores—and I'm not just talking about the aroma of dirty clothes sitting too long before a kid does something about it. I missed making things happen in the home that were gifts to my family.

How well our functional spaces actually function and how much we enjoy being in those spaces can determine how well we serve our families. We'll look at how textiles and fabrics, accessories, and architectural details can transform these areas in our homes.

Where to Start

Take a look at the spaces that work the hardest for you right now—your entryway, a mudroom, the laundry room, or maybe a pantry. Your house may not have these rooms, but you have spaces that serve these functions. So the question is, are they functioning

well? Many of the creative solutions that follow stemmed from needing more out of our old home (as in built in 1846!). More storage, function, and space.

My advice? Survey your space, and then start simple. This week, as you go about tasks in one of the utilitarian spaces, notice how it meets and doesn't meet your needs. We have a key hook with a mail bin hanging on the wall next to our door, so our car keys get hung immediately and the mail is stashed in a safe place. I can't tell you how many times I misplaced bills before finally designating a spot for the mail to sit until we have time to go through it.

What could be resolved with some planning and a few improvements? List your trouble spots and identify possible solutions. A catchall basket placed by the front door to collect items in a designated drop zone. Bins for shoes and hooks for jackets. See? Simple answers can bring order and peace to our homes.

Walls with Purpose
{Architectural Details}

Remember the kitchen wall I affectionately referred to as our wall of doors? The door to the right leads to our downstairs bathroom, and the door in the middle leads to our basement. But the door on the left leads to a small hallway and another door, which opens onto our backyard. At first glance, this hallway seemed completely useless. It's tiny—three feet by seven feet. So there wasn't any room for cabinets or a piece of furniture to create the additional storage we desperately needed.

This problem led us to a helpful solution. We decided to give this tiny hallway a purpose by recreating the look of an old schoolhouse coat room. We installed beadboard paneling three-quarters of the way up the wall and capped it off with trim molding. We painted it white and then hung two rows of coat hooks—an upper row for adults and a lower row for kids. This new coatrack wall system provided us with ample storage.

TIP

If space is tight, consider replacing a closet door with a sliding barn door for added visual interest.

A coat closet might have been the ideal storage solution, but we didn't have room for one, so we came up with a decorative way to hang coats that added a purpose for an otherwise unused hallway. This not only solved our drop-zone problem when we entered through the kitchen but also gave our kids a designated landing spot for their backpacks and jackets. Giving your kids a place for their belongings helps them get in the habit of putting their things away, which also means those objects don't end up on the floor for you or guests to trip over. Kids like having a sense of ownership with their belongings, and they are more likely to be consistent when they have a clear role in the family's team effort to keep the house clean.

At the bottom of our staircase at the front of the house, a small hallway leads to a tiny coat closet. We don't use our front door as our main entry, but we do use that coat closet to hold all our winter jackets. To spruce up the hallway leading to it, we installed a board-and-batten treatment to the walls, just like in our dining room and master bedroom. This addition of architectural interest made the hallway warm and welcoming. The ceiling light located at the bottom of the staircase was too far away to illuminate the coat closet, so to shed more light where needed, we installed two barn light sconces in the hallway above the board-and-batten. This brightened the closet and added some decorative task lighting.

The bigger rooms in our homes aren't the only places we can add architectural details. Adding wainscoting to a smaller room or hallway can be an affordable way to make a big impact.

I took the same approach in our laundry room. Even though our washer and dryer are hidden behind a curtain, I created a focal point by adding boards of reclaimed wood as a backdrop to our washer and dryer. We installed this accent wall in an afternoon, and it provides a delightful background, making the entire space more enjoyable for me every time I do a load of laundry.

TIP

You can also use wallpaper, a stencil, or installed tile to form an accent wall and create a focal point in your utilitarian spaces, bringing beauty into your everyday life.

A Warm Welcome

{Textiles + Fabrics}

We often bring area rugs into spaces to make them cozier or to ground the space. However, for utility spaces, we need to choose rugs that can hold up to extra wear and tear. Entryway and mudroom rugs are the hardest-working textiles in our homes. They are where we wipe our feet or stomp snow from our boots. Choose rugs made of durable materials. Outdoor rugs are nice and genuinely less expensive, but oftentimes their thin material cannot hold up in high-traffic areas.

I made the mistake once of choosing a thin cotton rug for our entryway, and it ended up in the washing machine more than on the floor because it could not hold up to our everyday use. I like to refresh our welcome mat a couple times a year, depending on the wear and tear. Usually every spring, once the snow and ice have all melted, putting a fresh welcome mat down is the first refresh I make for a cheery greeting.

Think about the rug needs for your space and your climate. Here in New England, our long winters turn into muddy springs, so I want my rugs to be practical as well as beautiful. Consider your region's weather when choosing the right kind of rug. I also like to keep a boot tray right by our entryway. Nothing protects your floors better than a convenient place to collect those muddy, wet boots.

In utilitarian spaces, floor-length curtains can get in the way, but that doesn't mean we should skip window treatments entirely. Try roman shades or woven blinds, which add texture in textiles without draping on the ground. Bamboo or wooden blinds that fit recessed within the window casings give the space a more custom look. This solution offers you the warmth your space needs while also looking high-end. When purchasing blinds to fit inside the window casings, size down by one inch. This will give you half an inch on either side, allowing you to

5 WAYS TO REFRESH YOUR SPACE ON A BUDGET

❶ Rearrange Your Furniture. This has been my go-to refresh since childhood! When you want a room to feel new, and before you consider shopping, rearrange the furniture. One piece or all the pieces. This can satisfy your longing for a change of view.

❷ Try a New Paint Color. The fastest and least-expensive way to transform a space is to paint. Going for cozy? Try a dark moody hue, such as Peppercorn by Sherwin Williams—one of my favorites. If you're ready for a breath of fresh air, use light and bright colors. Agreeable Gray by Sherwin Williams is lovely.

❸ Swap Your Furniture. Similar to the first idea, swapping select furniture pieces between rooms instantly refreshes multiple spaces. I do this whenever I want to shake things up, and it helps fight my urge to buy something new. You'll love the outcome of seeing your furniture in a new setting and light.

❹ Change Your Artwork. Do this seasonally or just because. The images and colors we hang on our walls have a big impact on how a room and its inhabitants feel. Changing up your artwork will help you reflect what you're currently loving.

❺ Create a New Vignette. Shop your home for the knickknacks to place in different rooms and groupings. This sheds new light on what you own and love. Consider buying a couple inexpensive new accessories to highlight the season of the year or a new color you're introducing.

open and close the blinds with ease. My favorite places to find affordable woven blinds by the inch are Overstock, Walmart online, and sometimes Amazon. Cordless blinds can be a little more expensive, but they are great at saving space and very easy to use, which can most often be worth the upgrade.

If your space is feeling cold, try warming things up with a new welcome rug or cafe curtains today. You just might be surprised at how these fabrics can soften and spruce up these areas, making them feel as pretty as they are practical.

Where Organization and Function Unite {Accessories + Styling}

Every item you bring in to serve a purpose can also double as decor. From the hooks you hang to the containers you add for storage, you can cater to your design style. Bring in your favorite colors and finishes with the color you paint the walls. Repeat or complement the finish on the light fixtures and hardware you choose. Just because these task spaces aren't the first places we think about decorating doesn't mean they should be the last place for beauty.

A piece of artwork, a plant, a lamp if your space allows, the hardware on the cabinets, or hooks you hang will reinforce your personal style. All of these details become the finishing touches that make the space attractive, homey, and inviting. Bringing in some design elements that were meaningful to me, such as favorite art prints, lighting, and some greenery, transformed the area into a space that was both functional and pretty—one that I actually looked forward to being in.

Think of areas you can add a quick fix to. Perhaps it's painting the interior of your front door a color for a bold pop. Or swapping out the ceiling light fixture for one that's embellished with crystal beads. Maybe it's adding some window treatments, such as roman shades. While these aren't the decor items you would typically

see on the shelves in a home decor store, they are ways in which we can add decorative finishes to a utilitarian space.

Don't forget about your organizational pieces either. Crates, baskets, and bins are all functional decor that give us closed storage that reduces clutter. When was the last time you cleaned out that hall closet? Or your pantry for that matter? Yikes! Before we start adding beautiful decor and figuring out what our storage needs are, we need to give ourselves a clean slate to start with. Going through our stuff and purging expired or unused items is a great place to start. Once we have cleaned out those closets or that pantry (or maybe both if we are being really honest), we can have a better idea of how to utilize the space and what we need for storage so that it is functioning at its best.

These utilitarian spaces, in-between hallways, and unused walls are all areas that offer untapped potential to lift us up as we serve our families better. With a little love and creative thinking, we can repurpose them into functional spaces that better suit our needs and tastes.

Have a blank wall you are tired of staring at? Add hooks that showcase your design style and create a place to hang your hat and tell your story.

The Family-Friendly Utility Room

The needs in your utilitarian spaces are bound to change with your seasons of life. Reevaluate how well your spaces are working for you, and make changes as your family grows. New season, new solutions.

To make up for our lack of a mudroom, we repurposed a wall in our kitchen to act as one. This was about helping the entire family . . . and more than a little bit about saving my sanity. In the kitchen chapter, I shared about adding a bench for the little ones to sit on while I tied their shoes and vintage crates below to organize those shoes. When my kids were old enough to tie their own shoes (hallelujah for new seasons of life!), a new issue emerged. They couldn't reach their snow gear, which I had in baskets on the top shelf of a closet. The bench in our kitchen was still functioning well, but it was no longer meeting our greatest need. I replaced the bench with a small dresser to hold hats and gloves and even some of the dog's accessories.

This simple change was just right for my growing family. Utilizing a dresser to hold their winter items meant fewer trips back and forth for me, while still providing a useful solution to keep all their gear organized and tidy. Once I reevaluated our current needs, I was able to outfit the space with the perfect solution.

Solving your family's storage needs shouldn't be overwhelming. Evaluate what items can be stored in their bedrooms, what needs to be kept by the door, and what is no longer being used. Are there enough coat hooks for everyone placed at the right levels? Decide where you want backpacks to be kept during the school year. If space allows, designate a bin for each child to corral seasonal pieces, such as winter jackets, boots, and gloves, and then rotate them out once it's time to wear sandals. This will keep your coat closet from overflowing. Sensible solutions can serve your family's needs during every season.

BRE'S TOP 10 ESSENTIALS

Baskets

Hooks

Plants

Artwork

Labels

Wall treatment
(for interest and reinforcement
for hooks and accessories)

Cubbies or lockers

Roman shades

Glass jars

Step stool

(diy) Driftwood Coat Rack

Whether it's salvaged boards from an old barn or pieces of driftwood found at the beach, I have yet to come across a piece of worn wood I didn't want to turn into something. My favorite something is a coat rack. These simple steps will help you create your very own with new or reclaimed wood.

SUPPLIES

- 1" x 6" pine board (or reclaimed barn wood or driftwood) cut to desired length
- Farmhouse hooks
- Stain color of choice
- Palm sander
- Drill and screws for hanging and mounting hooks
- Shellac or furniture wax
- Table saw

INSTRUCTIONS

1. Cut the board to your desired length. If you don't have a way to cut your board, most hardware stores can cut a board for you or may sell boards in shorter lengths, usually found on shelves below the longer lumber boards.

2. If you are using a new piece of wood, sand it down with 120-grit sandpaper. Apply your desired stain color and allow it to dry completely.

3. Once the stain is completely dry, apply a finishing coat of shellac or furniture wax to seal. If using shellac, let it dry and then lightly sand it with 400-grit sandpaper for a smooth finish.

4. Now you're ready to install the hooks. Mark the center of the board. Next, mark where your two outside hooks will go. (Do not place them on the very edge.) Then measure the distance between the middle of the board and the outside hooks, and mark even spaces where the in-between hooks will go. Install the hooks at all your marks.

5. Attach a hanger or picture wire to the back, and hang your coatrack in your desired place. Use anchors if you are planning on hanging heavier items, such as winter jackets or bookbags and heavy purses.

TIP

You can also use wallpaper, a stencil, or installed tile to form an accent wall and create a focal point in your utilitarian spaces, bringing beauty into your everyday life.

THE
FLEX SPACE

{ A Place to Create }

What is a flex space? It might be a bonus room, a loft, or the unused space above a garage—any area with multipurpose potential. That is a huge gift for a family or an individual journeying through the seasons of life. My hope is that this very moment might be the beginning of a season in which you can create a flex space that supports and encourages you. The best ones invite us to focus on a hobby, complete a project, or experiment with a new style. You might be able to use an entire room, or perhaps you can redeem one of your nooks or crannies. Maybe it is an angled hideout beneath the stairs or a closet that you've purged and cleared and prepped for something even better than storage.

When I was young, I pored over floor plans and imagined uses for rooms and nooks. As an adult, I still can't wait to look at a layout and envision how to decorate and design places that inspire daydreams and help people fulfill them. In my experience, flex spaces offer the most inventive interior design possibilities. What was once deemed the home office has now morphed into a more creative space that suits the needs of the entire family. One area can often be repurposed to serve the needs of several family members.

Not all homes have obvious flex spaces, but I believe we can all create spaces that offer us places to dream. To create. To explore. To feed our imaginations and interests. These are spaces where we can write, sew, scrapbook, create, work out, or enjoy quiet moments of reflection. The uses are unique to your needs. Whether you work from home, or you're turning a hobby into a business, or you're simply longing for a space to create, a flex space will give you the room to pursue your passions.

Having a flex space that serves our unique needs provides an opportunity to completely customize the way we style and enjoy it.

Two areas in our home serve as flex spaces. A small room off our dining room serves as our laundry room and doubles as a creative workspace/office for me. And we have a tiny room off our master bedroom that we walk through to get to the bathroom. Until I defined the purpose for the space, it couldn't become functional. Eventually, I envisioned it as a sitting room with two upholstered chairs and a side table. Now it is a quiet retreat for reading, journaling, and writing.

With a little imagination, we can breathe purpose into a space that is waiting to come alive. I've chosen furniture, texture and layers, and textiles and fabrics as my focus design elements. I hope you'll gather a few ideas to motivate and inspire your next steps.

Where to Start

Tour your home with the mindset of someone looking to buy it so they can have a couple flex space opportunities. I promise that you will notice a space you had forgotten about.

Perhaps it's a closet that could be better utilized as a craft space. An empty corner in your living room that accommodates a small desk and chair could create an inviting writing station. An attic

that can be turned into a yoga space or sewing room. Or a three- or four-season porch that can be transformed into an art studio.

Carving out flex space doesn't mean you have to surrender an entire room. Think about utilizing a landing at the bottom of a stairwell, or an empty corner, or window seat perhaps. Your space may be small, but that doesn't have to limit your creativity. Sometimes even a small space can provide the refreshment and creativity your soul needs.

What spaces of untapped potential are in your home? Once you've identified your flex space, you can determine how to make it function best to suit your needs. Loving our homes well means using them well so they can serve us to their fullest potential—and help us reach ours.

Get Clever for Comfort and Order
{Furniture}

Once you've identified the function of the flex space in your home, think of ways it could inspire your creativity and help bring your passions to life. Identify what your furniture needs are to help that space provide you the most function. Do you need a desk to write on? Or an easel to paint with? New cushions for your window seat? Sometimes I just long for a window where I can pull up a comfy chair, rest my coffee on a small table, and sit and read, journal, or reflect. Try thinking outside the box when it comes to adding office furniture. If it's a desk you need, look for antique tables or small kitchen tables for a uniquely sized and attractive option. They offer more work surface than a traditional desk and have a more relaxed feel. And such choices offer you more flexibility year by year should you want to shake things up every now and then.

When it comes to storage, consider an antique armoire or chest to hold all your painting or crafting supplies. Perhaps your room has space for a day bed that can offer comfortable seating and double as a space for overnight guests to sleep.

TIP

If your home doesn't have a flex space, designate a favorite chair as your place to reflect, read, or dream.

Clutter and visual distractions squelch my creativity, so I am intentional about keeping the clutter at bay. I like to incorporate pretty storage containers and baskets so everything has a home. Proper storage and an organized work space help you to think more clearly and stay on task without unnecessary diversions getting the best of your attention and time. Just like the other rooms in our house, if my office isn't clean and organized, it leaves me feeling anything but inspired to work.

Are piles of papers adding up around your home? Designate an area in your flex space that can help you organize bills and important paperwork so you can find anything easily when you need to. Perhaps lidded boxes or magazine files are the storage solution you need to organize your collection of craft books or cooking magazines.

I love to collect beautiful gift wrap paper and adornments. Nothing says "open me" like a beautifully wrapped gift, so I like a supply of pretty tissue paper and a variety of ribbons on hand. Keeping them in one place that's easy to get to, but kept out of sight in lidded storage boxes, preserves my creative space from becoming cluttered. I also like to collect antique jars to use as vases. Instead of taking up cabinet space, I store them in baskets in my office so that when I bring in fresh flowers to arrange, I can choose just the right vessel.

Personal touches, unique and clever furniture, and creative storage options give me joy. Decide what added features and furniture will allow you to walk into the nook or room and breathe a sigh of relief and delight.

The best flex spaces are the ones that serve more than one function and can adapt as the needs arise or as your family grows. Assess your space often to make sure it's serving your needs best, and don't be surprised if those needs change with the seasons of life.

Layering in a Comfortable Invitation
{Texture + Layers}

We touched on some furniture ideas already, but let's consider how your choices not only serve functions but also add interest and texture. Antiques are known for adding warmth with their weathered wood and worn or chippy paint finishes. That's why they are often my first choice.

The decor and furnishings you bring into your home tell a story, and that can inspire the choices you make. Antique or unique pieces bring layers and interest, adding their own story to yours the moment they land in one of your rooms.

If I'm not comfortable in a space, I probably won't want to spend much time in it. Choose your seating wisely. Chairs are one of my happy items to shop for and to add to a space. They add visual interest through their size, shape, and finish or upholstery. Wicker chairs can add loads of texture to any space. Sometimes a great accent chair is all you need for a focal point in your room or nook. Add throw pillows to create layers of comfort, and a chunky knit throw blanket for even more texture. Imagine your flex space as a creative retreat that draws you in and refuels your passions and desires. Gather items around you that will awaken your soul and spark creativity.

What are some of your favorite textures? Think of ways you can add them. Wicker, chippy white wood, and weathered wood are among my favorites, so I always look for ways to incorporate those, especially in spaces that I want to inspire creativity in me. Do you love a smooth, shiny finish? Try hanging or leaning a mirror in the flex space. Or perhaps an antique metal, like mercury glass candle votives. From the furniture to the light fixtures to the accessories, we can add texture and layers with the finishes we choose.

A layered room is an inviting room. It asks someone to stay awhile, look a bit longer, and take in the details that can surprise, soothe, or simply delight. What is more inviting than a space where we can be inspired and let our creative dreams run wild? Even if you are working with just a corner of a room, think about how you can add layers to make it feel cozy and truly usable. A few accessories might do the trick, like candles of various sizes or interesting bookends. A piece of artwork that welcomes your gaze could feed your daydream or showcase the colors that feed your spirit.

Sometimes our flex space is where we will display our favorite finds or keepsake items. It can become more intimate to us than other shared spaces, so why not give it visual texture and ambience with your nearest and dearest items? This can be the perfect place for your antique collection, a treasured vintage find, some framed family photos, shelved teacups, or a beautiful linen memo board to pin all your current inspirations.

Layering our flex spaces with pieces that inspire us and awaken our souls puts us in the right frame of mind to be creative. You be the judge (and shopper and decorator) to determine which textures and layers you can incorporate to transform what may have been an overlooked area into the place you can't wait to retreat to.

Showcase Personal Style
{Textiles + Fabrics}

When I'm imagining a space to offer me the utmost in comfort, I envision nice-to-the-touch fabrics and plush throw pillows . . . anything that will draw me in and encourage me to plop down and exhale. Adding in textiles, such as curtains, rugs, and throws, will reinforce the layers you've established and soften the space.

You would be surprised how quickly adding a rug and window treatments can transform a space. Try bringing in a small area rug to ground your space. If you are working in a corner of a room, a rug can define the area and distinguish it from the rest of the room.

What mood do you want for a flex area? Does it need to be streamlined to optimize productivity? Or do you want the mood to be contemplative? Creative? The style and fabric of the curtains you choose can become the backdrop for the mood you desire. Soft, flowing curtains that reach the floor offer a more casual vibe, while tailored, pleated curtains make a room seem more refined. If a romantic tone is what you're after, think about sheer panels with lace trim or ruffle detail, and let them pool on the floor. Ready for some drama? Choose velvet panels in a deep, rich color. Playing around with different curtain styles can help you achieve the look and feeling you want.

When coordinating different fabrics, I like to stay within the same color palette for a cohesive look. If I have soft white linen window panels for curtains, I like to bring in a white chunky knit throw and some white velvet throw pillows—all in the same color but different fabrics to add visual interest. This is also a fun way to add depth to a space. For instance, I love blue, so I will bring in different shades of blue—some navy, some chambray, and some pale blue—for a monochromatic touch of color.

Go back to your design style favorites. Which fabrics and materials are essential to your look, your tastes? Think of ways you can incorporate them, from upholstered footstools to the fabric on pinboards or memo boards used to organize the space. If an area feels too stark or cold, identify one or two places where you can add textiles and fabrics in your favorite colors and patterns to highlight your personal style and make the corner cozier.

When I say warm and cozy, by the way, what I really mean is whatever feels like home to you. My version of cozy might not be yours. You might like a rather empty canvas with only a couple of layers. Your best friend, whose style you love, might like many vignettes of layered textiles, art, and furniture that just wouldn't work in your home. Whatever you do, make sure the layers feel welcoming to you.

I can't wait to hear what dreams come to life as you begin to carve out a creative space in your own home today!

MY TOP 5 ORGANIZERS

❶ Baskets. With the right features, baskets are your organizational friend. Handles will help you move them around when they're full. A reinforced base and sides will improve strength and structure. Woven baskets without reinforcement will slouch or fall apart over time.

❷ Hooks. Make use of the vertical space on your walls or in closets. Hanging everything from totes to coats will make high-traffic areas more usable. Utilize wall space where shelves or baskets won't fit.

❸ Trunks. Whether wicker or wood, antique or new, trunks are ideal for storage and organization. Our kids' trunks hold large toys, such as Nerf guns, stuffed animals, and playtime costumes. The family heirloom trunk doubles as a coffee table in the living room and houses blankets and seasonal throw-pillow covers. Stuff remains tidy, concealed, and accessible.

❹ Small Dressers and Accent Furniture. Closets are hard to come by in our house, so I use antique dressers or accent pieces. These smaller choices tuck into corners, hallways, or stair landings and store hats and gloves, board games, toiletries, and much more.

❺ Drawer Organizers. Does your house have more than one junk drawer too? One day when I couldn't open a stuffed drawer, let alone retrieve something from it, I decided to purge one drawer each day of the week. I thought drawer organizers were for overly tidy folks, but it turns out they work fabulously. Years later, I'm happy to report those drawers are still organized and easy to open!

The Family-Friendly Flex Space

Friend, can I be honest? Sometimes I struggle with the idea of wanting a flex space. It seems selfish. Is it even worth the effort to create a space for myself? If I pause to let the truth emerge, I realize this: It's easy to become so consumed by caring for others that we forget to care for ourselves. If we focus only on others' needs for long periods of time, we end up putting our dreams and desires on the shelf. Or burying hobbies and hopes.

Let's allow ourselves the grace to pursue what sets our hearts on fire. I long for a space that reminds me of me. Where I can give myself the permission to dream again, be okay with mishaps or imperfect moments and rooms, because all such things add to our story and meaning.

As a creative person, one of the ways I recharge is by working with my hands. Painting a piece of furniture. Crafting a seasonal wreath. Doing an art activity with the kids or simply sitting with my journal and pen. When I'm exercising my creativity, free from distractions and unplugged from social media, my mind is renewed and my spirit refreshed.

Instead of viewing these spaces as expressions of selfish desires, we can see them as gifts we give ourselves to fill up our tanks so we can pour back into our families from a place of overflow instead of emptiness.

I believe that God placed passions on our hearts. Having a space to explore and express that creativity is one of the ways we can offer that gift back to him. Take a moment, grab a seat in a cozy spot, and think about what you loved to do as a child. You might be surprised by the dreams and passions that are still with you. Give them room to grow. Give yourself a room to grow in. The beauty that blooms will be a gift to your entire family. They may start hunting around the house for their own little flex space!

BRE'S TOP 10 ESSENTIALS

Comfortable seating

Inspiring decor

Bookcase or shelving

Decorative storage

Task lighting

Journal or planner

Books

Art or craft supplies

Desk

Plant

 # Pinboard

When I was in high school, I used to tape magazine cutouts to my bedroom wall, creating a life-size mural of anything that inspired me. Now, as an adult, having my own pinboard allows me the chance to get creative, and display the things that inspire my creativity the most.

SUPPLIES
– Corkboard (24" × 36"), hooks included
– Linen (one yard)
– Staple gun

INSTRUCTIONS

1. Prepare your fabric. (Iron out any creases before you begin!)

2. Lay the fabric facedown on your work surface.

3. Place the frame or corkboard facedown on top of the fabric.

4. Measure and mark the halfway points on both the fabric and frame.

5. Fold one side of the fabric over the corkboard. Starting in the middle, place three staples.

6. Fold over the opposite side, pull it tight, and place three staples.

7. Repeat for sides three and four. (Always pull tight before stapling it.)

8. Starting where the last staple ends, continue to staple the fabric along the edge toward the corner, stopping about 2" from the corner itself. (Keep pulling the fabric tight.)

9. Working clockwise around the corkboard, staple every other half side. (Pull tight!)

10. Working counterclockwise and starting from the middle, staple along the edges and stop about 2" from the corner. (Remember to pull the fabric tight!)

11. Finish the corners by folding the fabric around the corner edges and stapling it down.

12. Trim the excess fabric.

13. Nail the hooks into the back to hang.

14. Fill with inspiring images, textiles . . . whatever inspires you!

THE
KIDS' SPACE

{ A Place to Grow }

I have learned how to adjust our spaces over the years. I've also learned how to adjust my perspective on our kids' spaces and my hopes for them. Our children are now ten and twelve, and what they need in a creative space is different from what it was in the earlier years. At every age, I want them to feel they belong in our family areas and to know they have a personal area that encourages them, gives them comfort, and shines a light on their personalities.

I believe that every home with kids should have a space where the children feel truly welcomed to come as they are and grow into who they are to become. A place where their imaginations can fly freely, where they feel grounded in love and security. When we design a room or an area that inspires children to create and learn as they grow, we nourish who they are as individuals.

When you read the term "kids' space," is your first vision a messy room with germ-covered toys strewn corner to corner? I am here to help you claim a different vision—a much better one! I made that shift, and now I freely take steps to create places that foster my children's dreaming, playing, and opportunities to get lost in make-believe moments. And for a double win, I want that space to inspire me to embrace childlike joy, creativity, and the sense of possibility.

Kids' spaces don't have to be defined by their messes. Instead, let's define them as zones that give them permission to be kids. What could be more important? The area might be a cheery corner in your living room, their bedrooms, or a playroom if you're lucky enough to have the space.

Having a place to thrive and discover who we are provides comfort we all seek. Our kids long for that even if they can't put it into words. Designating a space where they can become who they are and celebrate their likes and dreams will, in turn, give us parents a little sanity through the messes and wild adventures that parenting can bring. Our homes are meant for living in, not being on display. Trust me, there have been plenty of times when I've had to remind myself to let them be little, to take a deep breath and focus on their excitement as they explore and learn in the safety of our home. I wouldn't trade that for anything . . . even a house that is tidy 24/7.

Creating space for their things is one way we can help ourselves not obsess about the mess. The other elements I focused on during my intentional pursuit of a kid-friendly home are furniture, color, and accessories. With childlike anticipation, let's look into the many ways we extend the gift of home to our very own children.

Where to Start

We can start our plan to designate areas for kids by identifying what they love to do. Do they like to paint or draw? Then perhaps a small table or desk in their room will give them space to get artsy. Do your kids love to look through books? Do they jump for joy when you suggest making forts with blankets draped over dining room chairs? Convert a corner into a cozy reading nook with a bean bag

chair, lots of throw pillows, and a fabric canopy to sit under. It will be their invitation to an adventure with their imagination.

You might have to surrender your design ideal for shared spaces. Sometimes I have to pause and let go of my need for perfection and allow my kids the opportunity to play freely while building memories regardless of the messes. (Yes, I just said that!)

Why do we embrace this shift? Because our kids are making memories, and I for one want to be a part of them. I bet you do too. These spaces become havens for our kids, so I want them to feel personal. Especially because of the fondness I had for my own bedroom growing up. After all, that's where my passion for rearranging furniture started.

Timeless Function
{Furniture}

When decorating my kids' rooms, I like to choose pieces that will work for them as they grow. Of course, my kids aren't still sleeping in their cribs! Once they graduated out of toddler beds, I began by using neutral colors for their bigger pieces of furniture. This way their furniture can suit them over time and give us longevity in the more expensive anchor pieces in their bedrooms. Choosing furniture in classic styles allows me the flexibility to change their accessories as they age without having to do the whole room over.

I stick to my design style staples that I incorporate in the other rooms throughout our house so that their bedroom feels consistent with the rest of our home. Sure, they have pieces in their rooms that feel personal and unique to them, but the main design in the room stays neutral, offering me the most flexibility with style pieces and accents that reflect them.

In our home, each child has a bed, a dresser, and a surface they can create on. I believe a space set aside for creative expression is so important. Our daughter loves to draw and craft. I found her an antique table that is smaller than a kitchen table but slightly larger than a desk. It provides her ample surface space for all her crafting masterpieces. Our son's room is smaller, so providing a surface where he can work was trickier. We built a custom farmhouse desk to fit his room. It is slightly narrower than a traditional desk and gives him space to build his LEGO creations or do schoolwork without taking up too much valuable floor space. Taking individual needs into account when furnishing our kids' rooms helped us to personalize each room. By giving them bedrooms where they can retreat to a place that's all their own, we provided a home base where they always feel welcomed to be themselves.

Selecting furniture that aligned with our kids' personal needs and preferences helped make their spaces feel more individual and also provided storage. This provided a huge payoff because their rooms stay cleaner—or at least their work surfaces do. Playful art and creative storage can help you display your child's favorite pieces, all while creating a room they delight in.

Think about the furniture in your kids' bedrooms. Does it function well to fit their needs? Bookshelves, step stools, and chalkboards are fun furniture pieces to incorporate into kids' spaces. Do they share a room? Are you tight on floor space? Then perhaps a bunk bed would be a better fit, providing more room on the floor to play.

Cohesive Welcome
{Color Palette}

Let's talk color! I know there can be a lot of questions about color in a kid's room, which is why I chose to include this design topic here. I tend to stick to neutral paint colors for the walls in our kids' rooms. Neutral doesn't mean only all white or all gray. Our son's room is painted Duke Gray, a medium shade of blue-green with gray undertones, and our daughter's room is painted Ella Rose, a soft blush pink, both from the Magnolia Home paint line.

Even though their rooms are painted pink and blue, the muted shade and undertones to these colors reflect a calming neutral base, which connects them visually to the rest of the home's aesthetic. By keeping their walls neutral, I gain the same benefit I do by choosing classic furniture: I get to bring in bolder tones and personality through the accessories and other details.

My kids love going with me to the paint store. They stand at the wall of wonder. You know . . . all those paint swatches revealing countless colors and variations. It is like the moment of bliss when they open a brand-new box of crayons, choosing the brightest colors that catch their eyes. Of course, that doesn't mean those colors will be going on their walls. I want my kids to be a part of the design process so they have ownership of their room and a partnership with me in the creation of that space. But I narrow down the choices before I show them.

For instance, for about a year, my daughter has been talking about wanting to repaint her walls (like mother, like daughter). Instead of taking her to the paint store and letting her choose from every color of the rainbow, I asked her questions first. "What color would you like to paint your room?" "Is there a particular theme or style you would like your room to represent?" "What rooms have you seen elsewhere that you love?" Asking her these questions first allows me to get an idea of some of the details she wants in her room. Then I made a solo trip to the paint store and chose a handful of paint swatches in the colors she mentioned.

By narrowing down her choices to ones I already approve of, she doesn't get overwhelmed by all the options, and we get to share in the design process. As for those bright colors represented on paint swatches she adored, I let those show up in accent pieces and accessories, like throw pillows, picture frames, or even a fun pattern in artwork. By controlling the narrative, you can be sure to create spaces that kids will love and that feel cohesive with your entire home.

Do you have a child who insists on bright walls? Choose a light shade of gray for three of their walls and then paint an accent wall the bright color. This can be a great way to create a focal point. If you're not quite sure how you feel about a fuchsia wall in a room, choose a piece of furniture to paint that color instead. Your kid, no matter their age, will love seeing their current favorite color gracing a dresser, nightstand, or bookshelf. This brings in the color your kid loves but on a smaller scale that won't take all the attention away from the other fun details in the space. Speaking of details, let's talk about those next!

Making It Special
{Accessories + Styling}

The kids' spaces I've seen over the years that grabbed my attention are filled with thought-out details that reflect the child who lives there. Choosing accessories and extras for your child's space is how you make it personal. I like to think of it as adding little gifts to their room that feel uniquely special so that opening their door is like opening a present. It draws them in with excitement.

I see the evidence of this when I've been shopping and bring home a trinket dish or a new throw pillow for my daughter in her favorite color. Her eyes light up as she sees new accessories in her room that make it feel special and personal. My son loves all things Star Wars. This is a six-year fascination, not a passing fancy. So I brought in artwork with a Star Wars theme—personal additions that gave him joy.

When our son was little, he loved playing with cars. He had a basket filled to the brim with various models of toy vehicles. In a matter of minutes, they would be spread out all over the first floor of our house. To encourage his creative playtime, we purchased a rug with a scenic design on it showing roads and parking lots. It was our way to cheer on his favorite form of play, and it created

a zone for that activity. And it reduced the number of times I stepped on a tiny car on my way to the kitchen.

Having your own special place helps you to feel safe and secure. And loved. When our children feel safe and seen, they blossom. It might seem like I'm giving a lot of credit to simple things like decor and colors and accessories! But think about the way your home, on its best days, feels like an expression of the real you. It creates a comforting sense of safety and belonging that inspires our spirits. We can help our kids have this too.

One way I make sure these blessings happen is by displaying special keepsakes. This is how we help our kids reflect their story. (Just like I love to do for our whole family, especially in the living room.) If you aren't sure what to include, consider pictures from summer camp, concert tickets, photos they took on their own, and pictures they drew or painted. Maybe you have a postcard from a special family trip. Any of these can be neatly displayed on memo boards for a personal and organized way to reflect the joy of their journey. Adding decor that reflects their hobbies or sports showcases their unique interests. Displaying these fun details highlights their personal style.

Maybe your child loves adventure and wishes for nothing more than to be outdoors or dreams of scaling a mountain or soaring down a zipline. You can find clever ways to bring those happy things into their room with details. Some common areas of interest include animals, activities, film or book characters and stories, sports, games, space, and the beach. Whatever captures the attention and heart of your child can be represented in their room.

The Family-Friendly Kids' Space

We have a small, odd-shaped room off our dining room where our washer and dryer reside. It's not quite big enough to be a bedroom, but when our kids were little, it was just the right size to be a playroom, with a door to close that could conveniently hide the mess.

TIP

Don't go overboard when decorating with a theme. A few key pieces can tell your child's story.

Perfect. Well, except that no matter how much I worked to make this confined space appealing, the toys wound up in the living room, where the kids wanted to be. The playroom dream I had wasn't an actual match for my kids, so I got to work incorporating pretty storage options for the toys and moved them to the living room. (Sigh.) When I occasionally had to step over toys, I reminded myself that soon my crawling toddlers wouldn't want to be by my side all day. I didn't want to wish away this time in their lives and mine. I embraced their messes, thankful that our children were learning and developing in a safe environment.

Do your kids love to be in the same room as you? Try designating an area that's just for them. Those storage baskets I mentioned were tucked around every corner of our living room for different activities. I had a basket with wooden puzzles underneath our coffee table. A basket for the train set was near the living room rug for easy setup and storage. There was even a basket for the plastic food that went with the play kitchen we pulled out during the day and then tucked away at night.

As my kids grew and their toys moved up to their bedrooms, I utilized the baskets for other things. I kept our living room flexible so that it would serve all of our family's needs. Embrace the mess, my friend, because I promise you the season will be over before you know it, and your kids will always remember the loving environment you created for them to learn and grow in.

BRE'S TOP 10
ESSENTIALS

Down comforters with
cotton duvet covers

Fun patterned sheets

Large baskets
(for bigger toys)

Bins (for smaller toys)

Blackout curtains
(perfect for nap time
or early risers)

A reading nook

Small desk + chair

Bedside lamp

Toy trunk

Memo or pinboard
(for displaying art
and keepsakes)

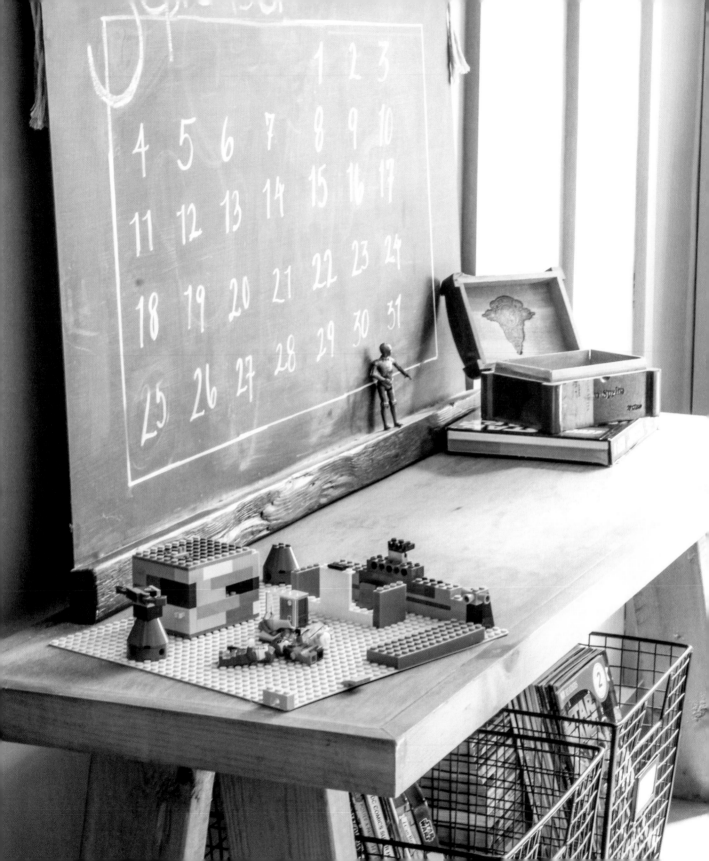

Kids' Farmhouse Desk

I mentioned that we made a custom desk to fit our son's small bedroom. We needed a desk that wasn't as deep as traditional desks but still provided ample workspace. We love how this little desk turned out, and it could even be used as an occasional table down the road.

DIMENSIONS
– 50" wide x 30" high x 15" deep

SUPPLIES
– (1) 2" x 4" x 10' board
– (2) 1" x 2" x 10' boards
– (2) 3/4" maple plywood project panel, 2' x 4'
– 1½" pocket hole screws (If you're not using a Kreg Jig to make pocket holes, use wood screws instead.)

– Kreg Jig
– Wood glue
– Stain color of choice
– Sealer

INSTRUCTIONS

1. Cut the 2 x 4s into four 29" lengths. Then cut all four ends at ten degrees off square.

2. Use the Kreg Jig to drill pocket holes on the outside of each leg at the top. This will create joints at the top of the legs where the desktop will be attached.

3. To make the tabletop, cut one piece of ¾" maple plywood to 14" x 49". On the bottom side of the desktop, use the Kreg Jig to drill two holes evenly spaced on each side. This is how you will attach the trim.

4. Cut two 1 x 2s to 50" length, and two 1 x 2s to 15" lengths, with an opposite 45-degree angle on each end. This creates a frame for you to trim around your desktop.

5. Attach the 1 x 2 trim pieces you have cut to the 14" x 49" maple plywood using pocket hole screws and wood glue.

6. Place the assembled desktop facedown and attach the legs just inside of the trim using the 1½" pocket hole screws and wood glue in predrilled holes.

7. To assemble the bottom shelf, cut the other piece of ¾" maple plywood to 13" x 38".

8. Cut two 1 x 2s to 39" and two 1 x 2s to 14" with an opposite 45-degree angle on each end. This creates a frame for you to trim around your shelf.

9. Attach the 1 x 2 trim pieces to the 13" x 38" maple plywood using pocket hole screws and wood glue.

10. Measure and mark 12" from the inside of the bottom of each leg. This will be where your shelf is attached. Using the Kreg Jig, drill pocket holes on the inside of each leg at the 12" mark. Attach the shelf using 1½" pocket hole screws and wood glue.

11. Stain the desk in the color of your choice and finish with a sealer. I chose to stain my son's desk Early American with a layer of Classic Gray (both by Minwax) lightly rubbed on top. (You can sand the 2 x 4 and 1 x 2 boards prior to staining, but the ¾" maple plywood does not require any sanding.)

THE
OUTDOOR AREA

{ A Place to Escape To }

Outdoor spaces offer a place to get away, even if only to our very own yard. At every home I've lived in, I occasionally pulled furniture outside to back porches, front steps, or a spot beneath trees to create a tiny outdoor oasis. A place where I could escape the household chores and actually feel off-duty, even if just for five or ten minutes.

Today, my family's favorite place to entertain in the summer is in our outdoor spaces. We love to share a meal outside with friends under the twinkling lights or sit around the fire talking the night away while our kids make s'mores. Here in New England, we are known for our long winters, with snow sometimes starting before November and lasting well into May. No wonder we make a dash for the door the moment it is warm enough to go on walks, work in gardens, or play games on the lawn.

I personally can't wait to get outside and feel the sun on my face as I tend to our outdoor spaces. I walk barefoot on the grass. I savor the smell and feel of soil beneath my hands as I pluck a weed or plant a bulb. These nature ventures in my own backyard allow me to tune out the distractions and burdens of the world and be soothed by the sounds of nature that calm my spirit.

Our yard didn't always offer a nurturing space to gather and just be. These spaces were carefully thought out and added over time. Our first priority was installing grass for our lawn. We moved from a city apartment, so our two kids, who were toddlers at the time, had the joy and gift of a yard. We were about to be thrown into landscaping 101. Over the years, through trial and error, we transformed our yard into the outdoor oasis it has become for our family and friends to enjoy today.

Because we were eager to get our patio area set up, I did a lot at once. It was therapeutic to be creating a space while fully immersed in nature. For our time together in this chapter, I will walk you through the three design elements that were most important. Furniture, lighting, and accessories and styling were the power three that turned a square of gravel into our oasis.

You can shape an outdoor space to extend your living area beyond four walls. I believe these areas can be just as warm and inviting as the indoor spaces we create. So if you have a patio, deck, porch, front stoop, or perhaps a blank canvas of a yard, I hope you will be encouraged and inspired to create an outdoor space that truly reflects you.

Where to Start

Start by identifying the natural elements that give you joy. What aspects of creation inspire you? Close your eyes and imagine you are outdoors in a setting that gives you pleasure and reenergizes you. Is there a shaded bench where you can sit and find relief from the midday sun? Do you smile at the thought of raised garden beds filled with fresh vegetables that invite you to get your hands in the dirt and participate in growing nourishment while being nurtured?

Is your imagined oasis the smooth terrain of a freshly cut lawn where you can play or simply gaze and exhale? Maybe you envision flowers gently swaying in the breeze, neatly tucked inside their hedged flower beds. Perhaps you see twinkle lights with their ambient glow echoing the stars of the night sky. Maybe your dream lands on the scene of rocking chairs arranged in a perfect spot for sipping lemonade on lazy summer days or a hammock tethered to two beautiful trees that offer shade and beauty. I breathe more deeply and smile as soon as these images come to mind. I smile with joy as I also imagine my family and your family discovering the gift of the outdoors in their own special ways.

Whether it be a balcony in the city or a backyard in the country, there's room for everyone to have their own personal outdoor oasis and to receive the gifts of nurturing and rejuvenation from creation.

Create a Cozy and Casual Space
{Furniture}

The key to creating an outdoor space you long to be in is to incorporate your favorite indoor comforts in a way that makes the most of the natural setting. When we first began cultivating our outdoor spaces, we didn't have any furniture that was intended for outside. One May as the ground began to thaw, we started dreaming up ideas of having our own backyard campfire area. With an upcoming commitment to host a Memorial Day barbecue, we got busy digging up grass where we would install crushed stone to help define the space. (By the way, if you need motivation to tackle an outdoor project, I highly recommend agreeing to host eight of your friends in two weeks!) The new gravel patio turned one corner of our yard into the outdoor fire pit area we love to entertain in. Now we just needed something to sit on and serve food on.

Don't have an outdoor dining table? Grab a coffee table from inside and bring it outdoors. Place pillows on the ground around it

---
TIP

Herbs planted in assorted pots make a great centerpiece for an outdoor dining area, one you can enjoy all summer long.

for a laid-back meal. I use old factory carts, sawhorses, or wooden crates turned upside down to create food and drink stations. Anything I can get my hands on with a flat surface might work to set food on. I always keep trays nearby for easy outdoor access to condiments and side dishes.

When thinking about seating for your outdoor areas, it's wise to plan on two to four more seats than the number of family members in your household. Since there are four of us, we wanted to get four more chairs so we could seat up to eight. An eclectic mix looks wonderful outdoors, so don't pressure yourself to buy pieces all at once. Take advantage of end-of-the-season sales to purchase outdoor furniture and add to your arrangement. If your area is uncovered, choose furniture made to withstand the natural elements so you can enjoy your selections year after year. Items that can be washed and wiped down easily will have longevity.

Get creative in repurposing furniture. There are no rules that say a piece of indoor furniture can't be the perfect choice for your outdoor area. And buying new is not always the best! Secondhand furniture is refreshed with a quick coat of spray paint. You can drape a colorful tablecloth over a long-used glass table for a new look. If you have an antique daybed that you rarely use anymore, bring it out to a covered porch. Could there be a more perfect spot for an afternoon cat nap?

Don't have a yard to play in? Furniture to the rescue! Set up tables and chairs on a porch, stoop, or patio where you can play board games and collaborate on puzzles in the fresh air. Or try out our favorite card game—cribbage. I grew up watching my parents play with relatives, and now my husband and I enjoy playing while sitting on our front porch.

Since creating our outdoor fire pit area, my entire family has become more appreciative of front-row views to creation. The farmer's porch that runs along the side of our house used to just be a place we passed through and got shelter from the rain when carrying in groceries from the car. Now it's furnished with a bench

and two rocking chairs, and I find myself retreating there again and again—sometimes in one day. It's my favorite spot to start the day with a cup of coffee or end the day with a glass of wine. It's the place my husband and I look forward to enjoying on the weekends, rocking side by side as we catch up from the week or share silence to reflect with gratitude on the blessings of our home and family.

Illuminate the Night
{Lighting}

I would bet a home decor shopping spree that lighting was not your first thought for a key outdoor design element. Yes, we typically use our outdoor spaces during the day when the sun provides all the light we need. But with lights, we can enjoy them well past sundown. When I wanted our outdoor fire pit area to feel cozy, I added lighting—string lights, to be exact. I knew the power of ambient lighting to transform a living room or bedroom, and sure enough, it did the same for this nook in our yard. Almost instantly our outdoor area was transformed into a cozy retreat by the soft glow of lights at dusk.

You might not need to use your lights all the time, and you may prefer to save them for parties. But I get so much joy from the gentle illumination, I pretty much consider them essential. You will be amazed at how string lights hanging low in an overhead tree or draped on a hedge of bushes can form the most beautiful backdrop for your next outdoor meal and inspire your next step in creating your own oasis. I encourage you to have fun exploring and incorporating different kinds of lights.

Clearly, string lights are my personal favorite because they offer the most flexibility. And let's face it—they are kinda magical. And these days, there are so many designs for strands of lights. You can find colorful, stylish, holiday-themed, and elegant options. There are exquisite ones with small bulbs tucked in metal figures shaped like a flower, bell, cross, or almost any other design you can imagine.

If you don't have an area where lights can be strung from overhead, fill vases or lanterns with battery-operated fairy lights. This allows you to have the same ambience when hanging lights or outlets are not easily accessible. Lanterns and candles offer a soft glow when placed along a center line of a long table or a perimeter glimmer when tucked around the edges of a patio or porch.

Create inexpensive ambient light with small votive candles placed inside mason jars. You can place them on tables or along pathways, or you can tie them with string and hang them from hooks or tree branches for a magical glow that lights up the night.

Whether simple or stylish, everyday or elaborate, lights will create the mood for your family dinner, girls' night, evening gala, or solitary quiet time under the stars. Even one lantern makes a big impact when brought into an outside "room." A glimmer of light has the power to transform a nighttime gathering into an enchanted evening.

Complement the Beauty of Mother Nature
{Accessories + Styling}

Honestly, I never really thought much about accessories for outdoor spaces until we made our gravel patio. Sure, I admired beautiful displays of outdoor furniture every spring in the department stores, but I never fully appreciated the impact accessories can have on an outdoor area until it was time to enhance the furniture we had chosen.

One spring my mom said she was gifting me a potted flower arrangement for an upcoming barbecue we were hosting. I thought it was a nice gesture, but it wasn't until she brought it over and placed on our outdoor table that I appreciated what a cozy addition a centerpiece could be. It's funny how plants can do that to outdoor spaces! Our property is surrounded by trees, but I

had never thought of the impact smaller potted plants could have. I have been a believer from that day on.

Potted plants will help you define an area, add in that cozy feel, and showcase a bit of your personality too. By picking plants in the colors we love, we add interest and life and style. I love the look of planters in different sizes and various species of plants nestled into corners. They add interest and depth with their colors, shapes, and sizes.

Accessories give us the freedom to create within creation. You might not display a rusted garden gate in your living room, but it can add dimension when displayed as a background structure for your flowers. Have fun with your accessories. Just like when styling inside, I create little vignettes around our patio and all along our porch. I like to make groupings of three, all in different heights. Planters in different shapes and sizes are a great way to do this and add dimension. If you want to add a little glow, throw in a lantern with battery-operated candles and a timer set for sunset. It's such a great feature, especially when you are outside enjoying your spaces and your lights turn on automatically.

Portable speakers and candles bring our indoor luxuries outdoors. Accessories don't have to be difficult. Choose ones that speak to your style in colors you like. Here's a fun tip—identify shrubs or flowers you love, and plant those in different areas around your yard for a cohesive look. It will center your overall outdoor space and create a casual, visual border to help make your primary outdoor space pop. There's no rule that says you have to mix things up. If you've found something that works for you and grows great in your climate, stick with it and delight in the ease of a beautiful, natural accessory.

The Family-Friendly Outdoor Area

We learned early in the parenting journey that if we had comfortable and engaging outdoor areas, everyone wanted to linger together in the fresh air. To shape a comfy area outside our home,

I decided to shop my home for the right pieces. I wanted a side table so I could rest a drink on it, some comfy pillows or a quilt to get cozy on the grass, and a portable speaker for music. You'd be amazed at how those few simple, everyday things create an inviting patio, porch, or other outside "room."

The minute we finished building our fire pit, our kids asked to make s'mores. Now I always keep supplies for s'mores in airtight containers so the kids can quickly grab what's needed. We've also served this favorite impromptu dessert many times to company.

What makes your family come together? Do you love playing games? Try your hand at building your own cornhole boards or a horseshoe area. Have you always wanted to grow your own vegetables but never got organized? Start now by growing a family garden together.

Not sure about your green thumb? Head to your local garden center and let each family member pick out their own potted plant. Read the planting instructions before you buy so you can determine whether your yard gets enough light. Once you have your hearty selections, use a family time to arrange the pots together. You can admire each person's plant as it grows.

My initial focus when creating inviting outdoor areas was on the memories to be made. The sweet bonus was that the spaces refreshed and nurtured me personally. They became true escapes for me and my family. Honestly, I had no idea how much I would love to tend to my plants or sit with my face to the sun.

Come savor the outdoors. The gift it offers isn't limited by the size of your space or what you have in it. A simple escape to a porch, gravel patio, or front stoop to breathe in fresh air, reflect on the beauty of a flower, or sit in a slice of sunshine will reap many blessings.

Galvanized metal buckets

Potted plants

Candles

Driftwood

Lanterns

Metal side tables

Watering cans

Trellis

String lights

Throw pillows

BRE'S TOP 10
ESSENTIALS

diy European Crushed Rock Patio

Our gravel patio emerged from our desire for a more useful, defined space. We didn't have the money budgeted to install granite cobblestone pavers as I had first envisioned, yet my search for ideas paid off. European pea stone or gravel patios fit the look I longed for at a fraction of the cost. Here is a step-by-step process for creating a space you will be grateful to add to your home and your life.

SUPPLIES

- Crushed stone of your choice—we used ¾" crushed granite. If granite is not available where you are, select ¾" crushed stone in the color of your choice.
- Bow rake
- Landscape fabric
- Edging of your choice
- Shovel and wheelbarrow (to use when clearing the area)
- Rented sod cutter (optional)
- Spray paint (optional)
- And my husband's favorite … music to work by!

INSTRUCTIONS

1. Spray paint lines on the grass or ground to outline the size and shape of the area you wish to dig out.

2. Either dig out the designated area with a shovel or rent a sod cutter to remove the grass. We have done both ways, and my husband strongly recommends renting the sod cutter!

3. Once the grass and debris are removed, spread landscape fabric down to help prevent weeds and grass from growing.

4. Determine which kind of edging border (if any) you want between the crushed stone and the grass, and install it. You can use rubber edging, plastic, or stone. Keep in mind that grass will try to take over, so having some type of edging in place ensures a crisp edge will stay intact.

5. Install crushed stone over the landscape fabric, spreading it out with the flat side of a bow rake, keeping the crushed stone to about 1½" to 2" thick. We had crushed stone delivered by the yard from a local landscaping company.

TIP

We learned that using the sod cutter removes the grass and leaves a nice smooth surface and straight edge to work with. If you cut sod by hand, you may need to rake out and level the area before moving on to the next step.

IT'S A GIFT

That environment you created, that space you cultivated, is a gift—even if you merely fluffed the throw pillows on your couch. When you take the time to make people (including you!) feel comfortable and welcome in your home, you are offering a gift for all to receive.

I hope this time together has inspired you to decorate your rooms with confidence and with elements that feel unique and true to you. May the home you create with love be the space you love to live in and give from every day. Enjoy it, my friend.

~Bre

RESOURCES

LIVING ROOM

sofa—Birch Lane

armchairs—Sixpenny

chest coffee table—Family Heirloom

rugs (both)—Overstock

curtains—Barn & Willow

curtain rods—Target

woven blinds—Lowe's

round mirror—HomeGoods

frames—HomeGoods

white lamp—HomeGoods

wooden table lamp—Target

floor lamp—Wayfair

round pedestal table—Amazon

round side table—Overstock

prints—Etsy

"By Wisdom a House Is Built" sign—Between
    Me & You Signs

throw pillows—With Lavender and Grace

coffee table tray—Amazon

wall color—White Heron by Benjamin Moore

DINING ROOM

table and bench—DIY

striped wicker chairs—Overstock

chairs with white slipcovers—Ikea

rug—Overstock

chandelier—Amazon

buffet—hand-me-down dresser

table runner—Not Perfect Linen

breadboards—Purple Rose Home

cow creamer—HomeGoods

woven basket—Farmhouse Pottery

maple syrup bucket—Antique

wall hanging baskets—Purple Rose Home

table lamp—Target

"Rooms for Rent" sign—Pottery Barn

candlesticks—Birch Lane

large glass vase—Pottery Barn

curtains—Tablecloths from Target

wall color—Peppercorn by Sherwin Williams
    and True White by Kilz with Magnolia Home

KITCHEN

bar stools—Ikea

runner—Target

pendant lights—antique

barn door—Artisan Hardware

tile floor—Floor & Decor

island countertop—Lumber Liquidators (DIY)

bench—DIY

crates—antique

"The Ache for Home" sign—Between You and
    Me Signs

galvanized bucket—antique
striped pillow—With Lavender and Grace
white enamel bucket (dog food)—Ikea
shelves and brackets—Home Depot
breadboards—McGee & Co.
cake stands—HomeGoods
white plates—HomeGoods and Ikea
glass canisters—Target
wall color—Gray Owl by Benjamin Moore

MASTER BEDROOM

headboard—Amazon
nightstand table—antique
nightstand dresser—secondhand
sconces—Birch Lane
ceiling light—Lowe's
rug—Overstock
frames—HomeGoods
prints—Etsy
curtains—Barn & Willow
woven blind—Overstock

Bedding

white quilt—Target
white linen duvet—Target
striped duvet and pillow covers—The Foundry
linen sheets—H&M
bed skirt—H&M
green lumbar pillow—Jolie Marche
wall color—White Heron by Benjamin Moore

BATHROOM

tile—Wayfair
dresser—Wayfair
wall sconces—Wayfair

rug—Home Depot
vanity—Wayfair
faucet—Wayfair
mirror—Wayfair
vanity light—Amazon
towel hooks—Amazon
shower curtain—HomeGoods
wall color—hand mixed: 75 percent Peppercorn,
  25 percent Revere Pewter

UTILITY SPACE

Back Hall Mudroom

wall hooks—Ikea
sign—DIY
hanging basket—Amazon
light fixture—Amazon
door color—Iron Ore by Benjamin Moore
wall color—Silver Chain by Sherwin Williams

Kitchen Entryway Bench Area

wall sign—Between You & Me Signs
bench—DIY
crates—antique
pillow—With Lavender and Grace
galvanized bucket—antique
wall color—Gray Owl by Benjamin Moore

Front Hall (By Staircase)

driftwood coat rack—DIY (hooks from Amazon)
sconces—Lowe's
framed art—Target
bench—DIY
light—Wayfair
rug—HomeGoods
wall color—Agreeable Gray by Sherwin

Williams

FLEX SPACE
Office Area
desk—Target
striped wicker chair—Overstock
lamp—HomeGoods
rug—Target
woven blinds—Lowe's

Sitting Area
chairs—Overstock
rug—Wayfair
round side table—Birch Lane
hanging wall art—Vol. 25
curtains—HomeGoods
walls—Stikwood Planks in Hamptons

GIRL'S BEDROOM
bed—Joss & Main
bedding—HomeGoods
throw pillows—HomeGoods
ceiling light—Pottery Barn Kids
bedside table—antique
picture ledge shelves—Ikea
dresser—Ikea
flower artwork—Minted
rug—Overstock
curtains—Wayfair
desk—antique
white wicker chair—Wayfair
"You are Made" Sign—Between Me & You Signs
wicker trunk—Ikea
wall color—Ella Rose by Kilz with
    Magnolia Home

BOY'S BEDROOM
bed—Birch Lane
bedding—Birch Lane
rug—Overstock
desk—DIY
desk chair—Birch Lane
dresser—Birch Lane
bedside lamp—Target
chalkboard—Antique Farmhouse
wall color—Duke Gray by Kilz with
    Magnolia Home

OUTDOOR AREA
Porch
bench—Overstock
planters—HomeGoods
hanging baskets—Home Depot

Fire Pit Area
sofa—Joss & Main
Adirondack chairs—Wayfair
planters—Wayfair
potting bench—Wayfair
terra-cotta pots—Michael's
garden stool—HomeGoods
concrete planters—Home Depot

Outdoor Dining Area
table—DIY
bench—Overstock
wicker chairs—Wayfair
white trellis—Amazon

About the Author

Bre Doucette is the author of *The Gift of Gathering* and creative founder and writer behind the blog *Rooms for Rent,* with its signature simple approach to design. She decorates with her heart and believes that whether you rent or own your home, whether you're an empty nester or a first-apartment dweller, you can love the space you live in.

In addition to being a wife and mom and writing her blog, Bre is passionate about creating beauty all around her in every aspect of life. Growing up in New England has shaped Bre's love for historic architecture, country settings, and coastal homes—all things that inspire her when she's creating spaces that are relaxed and comfortable with classic appeal.

Bre has been featured in *Better Homes & Gardens, Country Living, House Beautiful, Good Housekeeping, Yankee Magazine, Country Home,* and *Country Woman.* Her passion is to inspire women not only in their homes but also in their creative dreams. "Whether I'm decorating our home for my family or inspiring other women to enjoy their spaces, I love serving others through the gifts God has given me. Wherever you are in your journey, I hope you feel inspired and encouraged to embrace the gifts God has given you so you can bless those in your circles too!"

For more inspiration, connect with and follow Bre at
www.roomsforrentblog.com
Instagram @roomsforrent

Acknowledgments

To my *Rooms for Rent* blog readers. I never imagined that this amazing online community of like-minded souls would generate such camaraderie and encouragement. You gave me room to express my passion and helped me gain my confidence and find my voice in the design community. You helped this girl believe that she can help people love their spaces, even if she doesn't have a degree in interior design. Thank you for sharing in the joy and excitement of every project along the way. I will always remain forever grateful.

To Heather, for believing in me once again and seeing the vision of this book before it came to life. For knowing the encouragement it would be to others and helping me make this dream come true. To Hope, for coming alongside me in a crazy year and helping me put the expressions of my heart down on paper. And to the team at Harvest House that made this book a reality. Your time and effort and creative vision for this project blow my mind, and I am beyond grateful for all you've done to make this book a reality. I can't wait to hug each and every one of you someday!

To my mom, for showing me what it's like to have a warm welcome to come home to and a soft place to land. For all the countless hours you spent making our home lovely so we could all feel welcomed, and for tangibly showing me the gift of hospitality.

For every single family member and friend who stood by me and encouraged me as I wrote this book. For helping me with the kids, sending me your prayer texts, and providing constant support...this book would not be here if it weren't for you. Thank you!

From the bottom of my heart...I can't thank you all enough!

Cover design by Nicole Dougherty
Interior design by Faceout Studio
All photography by Bre Doucette

Ten Peaks Press is a trademark of The Hawkins Children's LLC. Harvest House Publishers, Inc.,
is the exclusive licensee of the trademark Ten Peaks Press.

The Gift of Home
Copyright © 2022 by Bre Doucette
Published by Ten Peaks Press, an imprint of Harvest House Publishers
Eugene, Oregon 97408

ISBN 978-0-7369-8151-4 (hardcover)
ISBN 978-0-7369- 8152-1 (eBook)

Library of Congress Control Number: 2021939151

Printed in China

21 22 23 24 25 26 27 28 29/ RDS–FO / 10 9 8 7 6 5 4 3 2 1